£1-25

The Geography of
British Heavy Industry
since 1800

KENNETH WARREN

and Practice in Geography

OXFORD UNIVERSITY PRESS · 1976

Oxford University Press, Ely House, London W. 1

GLASGOW NEW YORK TORONTO MELBOURNE WELLINGTON
CAPE TOWN IBADAN NAIROBI DAR ES SALAAM LUSAKA ADDIS ABABA
DELHI BOMBAY CALCUTTA MADRAS KARACHI LAHORE DACCA
KUALA LUMPUR SINGAPORE HONG KONG TOKYO

ISBN 0 19 8740379

Printed in Great Britain
by J. W. Arrowsmith Ltd., Bristol

Preface

Although the 'classical' Industrial Revolution of 1760 to 1830 has long
attracted the attention of economic historians, the last decade has also
brought innumerable analyses of the developments of the British economy
in the later nineteenth and the twentieth century. With occasional exceptions economic geographers have tended to avoid this period; a few
excellent surveys have been made, but none which stresses factors rather
than individual lines of economic activity or which aims to relate the
past to the present and to contemporary economic problems. My aim
has been to emphasize the dynamism and change, the throbbing development of location patterns in the Victorian free enterprise economy
which, for a variety of reasons, led in the twentieth century to a growing
ossification in the patterns of heavy industry. In tracing this movement
I have tried to balance the more limited concern of the academic against
the wider interest of the applied geographer in modifying the actual
spatial organization of activity for the benefit of society. Economic
geography should never be content to be merely academic—its part in
understanding and remaking the world is far too vital.

Witney, Oxfordshire   Kenneth Warren
Easter 1975

Contents

1 Introduction

Economic geographers analyse the spatial patterns of economic activity which diversify the surface of the earth. Generally speaking, these patterns are the product of attempts to satisfy the extraordinary variety of human wants with as little effort as necessary. The distribution of economic activity is not static, and the so-called Industrial Revolution, whose impact was first felt in Britain some two hundred years ago, has transformed it more rapidly and more completely than ever before. The effects spread to all economic activity and indeed to society, politics, and the whole of life, and, in addition, from Britain the effect spread throughout the world. A limited group of manufacturing industries played the role of a leading sector in this transformation. A very prominent member was the textile trade, which is not considered here, but the heavy industries were also at the centre of the industrialization process.

In the past the entrepreneur, the initiator of the industrialization process, has usually been depicted as an 'optimizer', that is, he was believed to be concerned to minimize costs and maximize returns. To this end he endeavoured to find the best combination of the factors of production both in terms of amount and of location. Capital and labour are mobile but land is fixed and therefore the costs of assembling raw materials and distributing finished products has traditionally occupied the central place in the study of industrial geography. Commonly, too, location study has been atemporal. The result of these conceptual limitations was a failure on the one hand to recognize that capital, labour, and entrepreneurship were by no means wholly mobile, and on the other that locations, once chosen, were very frequently perpetuated into periods when technological and market conditions had changed.

Belatedly, in the last decade, explicit recognition has been given to the importance of these considerations, long recognized in specific studies but not comprehended by location theory. Following the 'behavioural revolution' we now recognize that entrepreneurs, whether private or state, are not in full knowledge of the conditions which will affect their operation, do not operate on purely economic principles in making decisions on the basis of this knowledge, and are not concerned to maximize profits anyway—three situations which may be summed up as 'partial knowledge', 'bounded rationality', and a 'satisficer' rather than 'maximizer' motivation. The result is a 'suboptimal' locational choice or location pattern. In fact the industrial geography of any advanced country consists of regional associations of suboptimally located manufacturing operations. These are passed on from each generation to become the planning problems of the next. Modern industrial Britain, problem-ridden as it most obviously is, exemplifies this particularly well. A mature industrial economy cannot erase the past and build anew. Past location thinking and practice have not only shaped the present but also limit the freedom of contemporary planners to remake the geography of industry.

The last new major districts in British iron- and steelmaking, Lincolnshire and the coastal districts of Cumbria, took shape one hundred years ago. At the same time Barrow in Furness became the last important new shipbuilding district. In chemicals there have been much greater changes but Runcorn-Widnes, where development began over 120 years ago, is still a major centre of activity. Generally the conclusion which emerges from a study of British heavy industry is that the ease with which locations change decreases over time. This is a fact of immense practical significance.

The literature of the last century—at a time when scale economies were not yet big enough for expansion of existing plants to meet demand and when new mineral districts were being opened—contains many accounts of industry springing up in remote locations, converting farmland into factories, populating the waste and, generally in accordance with Victorian canons, leading to 'progress' even if the new cultural landscape was less picturesque than the old one. As late as 1903 Sir Hugh Bell, in whose childhood the first ironworks were being built on Teesside, anticipated that these changes would continue. 'The iron trade', he wrote, 'has again and again changed its habitat in Great Britain, and, unless I am mistaken, will change it again and again in the future' (Bell 1903). Events proved Bell mistaken for not only have no completely new districts been added but in the following seventy years the number of completely new greenfield sites was confined to three— Normanby Park (Scunthorpe) and Irlam, Lancashire, just before World War I, and Newport, Monmouthshire, in 1962 (at Corby and Port Talbot there were already some metallurgical activities on the site). A quarter of a century after Bell Lord Aberconway traced out the growth phase of British heavy industry in which '. . . collieries, iron and steel furnaces, foundries, forges, engineering plants, shipyards, sprang up in our midst' and although he recognized that he wrote in a time of crisis he did not seem to anticipate the elimination of scores of these units which occurred in the next few years (Aberconway 1927). Yet many of the old plants still survive and the location pattern of these industries is still recognizably close to that of the 1920s or even earlier.

However, the geography of industry is concerned with much more than a narrow locational analysis. In the process of growth, changing locational influences, and the establishment of new or the closure of old plants, the situation of individual works and whole districts changes, improving or worsening as management seizes or lets slip opportunities, as it reacts positively to challenges or watches inactively or perhaps impotently as both dividends and work forces decline. Locational change has even wider significance for regional, national, and, as when Britain was the only industrial nation, international geography is changed as well. The numbers, occupations, and social status of the people change, transport and communications establish new space relationships with other areas and the landscape is transformed. All this is part of the perspective of the geographer, who, while focusing on location and locational change, is yet concerned with the wider context and effects. As Hartshorne argued long ago, the geographer is concerned with the areal significance of the industry, not merely with its location (Hartshorne 1939). A still wider aspect neglected by geographers, which cannot be explored at any length here, concerns the reasons for the changing international role of Britain and focuses on her heavy industry as part of the location pattern of world manufacturing.

Study of the geography of heavy industry over more than a century and a half provides a series of extended test cases of the working of location theories. On it has also depended the reshaping of the human geography—the wider economic, social, and even political aspects—and to a not inconsiderable degree the physical geography of Britain (Wallwork 1974). Finally, in an era of awakened social conscience, old location patterns are not easily remade. Britain's nineteenth-century heritage constrains contemporary freedom to plan for A.D. 2000 and beyond. Some of these themes are explored below—selectively and briefly but none the less with the aim of clarity and cohesiveness.

Heavy industries: definition and characteristics

It is not possible to fix tidy limits to the field of heavy industries, but the broad scope is clear enough. The words 'heavy industries' are not directly interchangeable with 'basic trades' and still less with 'staple industries'. Basic trades include coalmining, whereas the intention here is to focus on manufacturing—though a hundred years ago the distinction was less clear than now because of the areal and organizational links between the two. Staple trades include the textile industries in nineteenth-century Britain and the motor industry and other industries manufacturing consumer durables at the present time. The term 'heavy industry' implies either bulk-reduction processes which are usually, though not invariably, mineral based, or the further processing of heavy products from these primary stages of manufacture. Two mineral-processing industries stand out as of prime importance—iron and steel and heavy chemicals. Non-ferrous metal processing is locally but not nationally important and is not discussed here. The further-processing industries include heavy engineering and shipbuilding. Within industries and even more within the larger individual firms it is always difficult, and sometimes impossible, to draw a workable boundary around heavy industries, the point at which, for example, heavy chemicals pass over into fine chemicals or when heavy engineering becomes light.

Early location theory, and most notably Weberian analysis was pre-occupied with heavy industry. Characteristic features are bulk reduction, implying considerable loss of weight during manufacture, but also a bulky and often low-value product for which it may be extremely difficult to establish consumer preference. Raw material, and above all coal-field orientation, is indicated by the first characteristic. Until the introduction of the hot blast in 1828 as much as 8 tons of coal were used to make 1 ton of Scotch iron. In the late 1840s Tyneside's chemical industry produced annually 60 000 tons of saleable products but in that activity used 15 000 tons of sulphur and nitrate of soda, 42 000 tons of salt, and 153 000 tons of coal or coke, giving a material index of 3·5 (*Mining Journal* 1850). Shipbuilding, as an industry concerned with the putting-together of sub-assemblies and with a limited range of sites, clearly differs in its locational conditions from the heavy bulk-reducing industries, but in the nineteenth century proximity to sources of iron and steel, and perhaps still more to numerous component trades, provided an important locational consideration.

The second leading characteristic of heavy industries, bulky, low-value products, emphasized the desirability of regional sources of supply at a time when processes were inefficient and above all fuel intensive, and when land transport was still sometimes difficult. The widespread distribution of British coal reserves helped to diffuse industrialization throughout the country before the extension of the railway network in the 1840s made movement between regions practicable in addition to the coastwise movement which had long been important. The difficulty of establishing consumer preference and consequent sharp price variations as supply and demand relationships changed led to an early stage to attempts to regulate output and price by trade-wide meetings, eventually to more formal organizations, and then to big regional or national firms or countrywide associations.

Because of the weight and size of materials and products handled, or because of their high temperature or dangerous chemical characteristics, there was much pressing for mechanization in the heavy trades. This often resulted in large capital investment by the standards of the time and to large-scale production in order to take full advantage of the machinery. Scale economies in individual units of equipment implied, with their combination into works, big operations and, therefore, in spite of the capital outlay, large work forces. It is true that there were exceptions, the West Midland sheet iron trade, for instance, being one into which entry was cheap even into the last decades of the nineteenth century, and in the 1880s it was said that in Yorkshire and Lancashire a chemical firm was little more than 'a couple of carboys and a stink'.

Frequently, recognizing common gain from the availability of local resources or nodality with respect to common services or materials, various trades swarmed in particular areas. The result was not only external economies from the grouping of like businesses in a particular area but also big urban agglomerations with all their environmentally harmful accompaniments. There were exceptions such as the scattered centres of the Ayrshire or the Northamptonshire iron industry, chemical manufacture in Flint or in rural Worcestershire, or agricultural machinery production in the market towns of eastern England, but generally heavy industry with its interlinkages, and above all its close relationship with coal production, built up great industrial/urban complexes. In some cases these were in areas which would not otherwise have been settled on any large scale. Teesside was one example, but this was epitomized even more by the iron towns of the north crop of the South Wales coalfield. Here where an astonished American ironmaster noted 'the human mind is lost in wonder at the combination of material and intellectual elements required for the organization and conduct of such gigantic operations . . . ' (Hewitt 1868) a natural wasteland was peopled. Merthyr, the metropolis of this belt, was a mere village in the 1750s. Between 1759 and 1782 four ironworks, Dowlais, Cyfarthfa, Plymouth, and Penydarren, were established nearby. By 1901 the population of the town was 69 000, which was 20 000 more than Newport and 42 per cent of the population of Cardiff. Merthyr's growth and the crisis which followed the collapse of its puddled iron trade in the 1870s highlight the fact that generally in the *laissez-faire* Victorian climate of opinion industrial locations and the populations which they aggregated rose and declined with the minimum of interference. The process was painful to individuals and to communities, but this was the price of progress, something mechanistic, part of the order of things. As the General Manager of Palmers of Jarrow concisely summed up the philosophy behind it in the mid-1880s, 'we have two divisions of plant, living and inanimate, machinery and men' (Price 1886). However, as will be seen below, this did not prevent some Victorian 'captains of industry' from struggling to preserve locations whose advantages had declined. In the twentieth century as capital outlay on new plant, particularly on completely new sites, has risen, so it has become less easy, for purely economic reasons, both to abandon old locations and to develop new ones. Social and political action has progressively reinforced this growing commercially based reluctance for locational change. Most important of all, government, always indirectly involved, has become directly concerned in industrial location as the most important element in its regional policies.

In the nineteenth century most industry was regional, in its materials, in its markets, and therefore also in its perception. It is true that in addition to their regions British heavy industries looked outward to the world markets and that there were connections between regions long before this. In the nineteenth century the number of regional interconnections multiplied—Tennants of Glasgow built alkali works on the Tyne, Black Country firms invested in the iron industry of the North East or in Scunthorpe, Teesside capital was invested in mines and works in South Wales, and so on. Even so, regional markets were reflected in regional specialization and in the way in which consolidation of firms also generally took place only within one region. In steel this led to very marked regional product specialization which still survives, such as sheet and tinplate in Wales—exceptional in that the market was not in the same region—plate and angles in central Scotland and the north east of England, tubes in Lanarkshire and the Black Country, wire in south Lancashire. In later rationalization programmes this led to the perpetuation of old patterns on the very doubtful principle that there were 'proper places' for particular trades (Warren 1970). The landscape of heavy industrial districts was shaped by the business philosophy and master/man relationships of the great expansion phase. Now, once booming industrial areas are variously but hideously scarred—the stranded communities and hillsides malformed by the remnants of old mineral working along the North Crop, the widespread dereliction and scattered small Lanarkshire mining and ironworks settlements viewed from the banks of the incised river Calder, the prospect from Scotswood bridge of the old-style, dark industrial structures where Lord Armstrong and his successors made their money at the cost of unknown thousands killed or maimed all over the world and which are now decaying into a dirty, grossly abused river, or the grim grid-iron pattern of housing and the still awe-inspiring shipyard core which Vickers built up in Barrow. These are not just landscape features fascinating to the artist or the geographer with a rather odd sense of values, they are part of the physical planning problem of these areas today and substantially affect the assessment made by entrepreneurs of regional prospects. Already by the interwar years the unsightly relics of the old Tyneside chemical industry were believed to be an obstacle to redevelopment and the introduction of new industries. It is true that in some cases landscape impressions may be deceptive and that, other factors being favourable, diversification may flourish in a most unsightly setting. At the end of the nineteenth century an American wrote that the Black Country '. . . has long since had a worn-out appearance—effete they would call it in Chicago' (Mattox 1898), but the seeds of the twentieth-century boom in the West Midlands industries were in fact already taking root in this most umpromising-looking soil (Allen 1929). Generally, however, either the 'burned out' industrial enterprise of the old heavy industrial districts or their perceived, that is their believed, unsuitability for modern development is a formidable problem, as the emotive force of such names as Coatbridge, Jarrow, or Merthyr Tydfil shows. Furthermore, it is not merely physical inheritance which is such a problem, there is the legacy of old frameworks of thinking, of the relationship between management and men, of attitudes to work and to innovations. Sometimes they are, more often they are assumed to be, inimical to economic progress. In this less tangible, but all too real, way the geography and the history of heavy industry confound today's regional planners of late twentieth-century Britain.

General themes: growth and industrial 'heritage'

Britain as the first industrial nation has paid dearly for the honour. Indeed it may well be argued that interwar, and still more, post-1945 efforts to modernize and make a truly viable national economy have ended in the frustration and recession of the mid-seventies because there was a failure to face up to the fact that Britain was attempting something uniquely difficult, nowhere else so serious. That task is to remake an economy and economic and social relationships which, more than in any other country, were shaped in the nineteenth century.

No major new shipyard has been built in Britain for over fifty years. It is true that existing yards have been reconstructed and re-equipped on numerous occasions, the old smaller slipways being merged or re-aligned, and that formerly independent neighbouring yards have been combined, sometimes, as was the case in 1974 with the Wear yard of the unfortunate Court Line, being levelled and completely rebuilt, but such developments change site conditions and they do not affect the wider issue of locational values. No greenfield site, no completely new location has been started for British shipbuilding since the spate of new yard construction which accompanied the German submarine campaign of the last years of World War I reached completion in the early 1920s. Earlier, at a time when growth of shipbuilding was more rapid, the scale of plants much smaller, and Britain's supremacy in building seemed secure, the location pattern of the industry had been much more fluid.

Most of the new yards were built on the rivers of the North East coast or on the Clyde and it was in these areas that shipyards were most fully part of what might be called a shipbuilding complex—plate and angle mills, engine works, steel founding, and the extraordinary diversity of supply trades. As new yards were opened new urban/industrial centres developed. Thus, for instance, the area of the burgh of Clydebank was almost wholly rural until the late 1870s when major shipyard activity began at Yoker, Clydebank, and Dalmuir. By 1901 the burgh contained over 21 000 people. By that time the availability of a large potential work force had brought the Singer Manufacturing Company to Kilbowie where it employed some 7000. Down the Clyde at Greenock the Scott's yard is claimed as the world's oldest, dating from 1718.

The important yards on the Irish Sea at Belfast, Birkenhead, and Barrow were developed later than the Scottish or North East England ones and never developed such a major regional supply network. They have survived to the present day on large supplies of material from other regions—in ship plate, for example, Wednesbury is an important supplier to Birkenhead and the Clyde has always dominated the supply to Harland and Wolff.

Location and site sizes appropriate in the nineteenth and early twentieth centuries are clearly not ideal in an era of supertanker construction. Small operating scales in the past led to a proliferation of units which still makes rationalization into a world competitive industry difficult. Even so a great deal has been done. In the early 1920s the Tyne, Wear, and Tees had forty shipbuilding firms. There are now only three important concerns (Aberconway 1927).

Less has been inherited in chemicals, for products, materials, and technology have changed to a much greater extent. The big new petro-chemical complexes, for example at Baglan Bay, Grangemouth, Ellesmere Port or Immingham now outrank many of the older chemical agglomerations, but in spite of a revolution in processes and a new, vastly greater order of production the two greatest regional concentra-tions of heavy chemical manufacture are now, as one hundred years ago, Merseyside and North East England. In detail the legacy of the past is still significant. Into the 1950s the largest production of sulphuric acid in Scotland was at the I.C.I. installation at St. Rollox in East Glasgow where Charles Tennant built his great bleach works in 1798. There is no remnant save in waste heaps or in place names of the great Tyneside alkali industry of Victorian times (Campbell *c.* 1965). The links of the chemical industry of modern Teesside cannot be traced back earlier than the opening of the saltfield there in the mid-1880s. Runcorn, Widnes, and above all St. Helens take the story much further back, in the case of St. Helens to the establishment of the glassworks at Ravenhead in the 1780s. The Victorian legacy of heavy chemicals on Merseyside is not only to be seen in the dereliction along the Sankey Canal or in the drab housing and street names so evocative of the early Leblanc pioneers in Widnes but also in current major employment and in expenditure by I.C.I. and Shell which has grafted new petro-chemical growth points on to the old coal- and salt-based structure.

Iron and steel has a larger heritage than chemicals in individual plants as well as districts. Even now, when the British Steel Corporation Devel-opment Strategy (B.S.C. 1974) contemplates more radical reshaping than ever before the past cannot be shaken off and has indeed animated pressure groups which through parliamentary decision have suceeded in redeeming a number of plants which B.S.C. planned to close. The Development Strategy provided for five integrated steel operations by the early 1980s with a combined ingot steel capacity of 30 million tons or some 84 per cent of the national total. The largest of these, Lackenby-Redcar with a capacity of 12·5 million tons, will have its own deep-water ore dock—already in operation—and occupy an excellent site, one com-pletely undeveloped until the late 1940s though lying between the site of the Eston Junction (now Cleveland) Works built in the early 1850s and the site of the three ironworks of Lackenby, Coatham, and Redcar built in 1871, 1873, and 1874 respectively. Port Talbot works spreading over the former sand dunes of the eastern side of Swansea Bay and also possessing a new deep-water dock, will be extended to 6 million tons but this plant is the direct descendant of a series of works which stemmed from the decision made by Miss Talbot in 1899 to develop land which she owned there. Ironworks were in operation at nearby Taibach in 1750, there were blast furnaces there in 1811, and between 1820 and 1835 iron plates were made at Cwmavon. The Newport works to which B.S.C. is to make smaller extensions occupies a site which was wholly undeveloped until 1959. The other two sites for expansion are Ravenscraig near Motherwell and Scunthorpe.

Scunthorpe is 22 miles by rail from the new ore dock at Immingham, Ravenscraig 17 miles from the present inadequate dock at General Terminus Quay, Glasgow, and some 48 miles by the shortest route from the giant new dock to be built at Hunterston on the Firth of Clyde. Ravenscraig lies to the south of the great boom area of Scottish blast furnace construction of the 1830s and 1840s but within the area of forge and steelworks building of the following two generations. At Scunthorpe iron was first made in the mid 1860s and steel in 1890.

By contemporary world standards only Lackenby-Redcar, Port Talbot, and Newport are ideal locations for large-scale bulk steelmaking operations and Newport only if it is provided with its own ore dock. The nineteenth-century heritage is much more prominent in other works still supporting large populations and some of them saved from the winding-down which B.S.C. proposed. Examples (with their dates of construction) are Shotton (1896), Cardiff (1890), Consett (1840), Shelton (1832). In other instances the ancestry is still older as with Clydebridge/Clyde Iron where ironmaking began in 1786, at Ebbw Vale where the first blast furnace was built in the 1780s, or at Bilston just south of which, at Bradley Hall Fields, John Wilkinson acquired interests in charcoal blast furnaces in the early 1750s. These seven works alone produced 5·7 million tons of steel in 1967 (Table 1).

TABLE 1

Age and steel production of the 22 British integrated steelworks 1967

Date of establishment as metallurgical site	Number of works	Production 1967 (th. ingot tons)
Before 1800	4	2812
1800–1850	3	1747
1850–1900	9	8121
1900–1930	4	4273
1930–1950	1	1008
1950–1967	1	1473
	22	19434

Sources: Age of works, various; production, British Steel Corporation.

The unique and national planning

The geography of British heavy industry today is the product of the working-out of demand, material supply, and technological changes in a unified national economy. In the past in studying this geographers may well have paid too much attention to finer details, for instance to the peculiar influence of geology or the chemical composition of ores, thereby losing the wider perspective. Too much attention has been paid to appearance and structure, too little to flows and relationships between districts. Nowadays, by contrast, geographers are in danger of concentrating too much on likenesses between regions, too much on the inter-linkages between industries and too little on distinctive characteristics. Many themes of development are common to the heavy industrial regions but they each have unique variations. In making modern geography more analytical it is vital that the unique element should be kept in view. If it is not, general policies will be applied in circumstances which demand special treatment. Problems will be misinterpreted and solutions will be inappropriate. Even though it may be less important, the future pattern will have the grey drabness of greater uniformity as compared with the fascinating variations on common themes which still give so much flavour to the study.

2 Location choice and locational values: theory and practice

Both Von Thunen (Hall 1966) and Alfred Weber (Weber 1929) produced highly simplified models for the study of the location of economic activity. Process costs were initially assumed to be equal everywhere. Distance and movement costs were reckoned the most important variables between different locations. Entrepreneurs were assumed to be fully aware of the cost situation and to act rationally in their locational responses. It is now widely recognized that each of these assumptions was incorrect (Smith 1971; Collins and Walker 1975). Study of heavy industry in the nineteenth and twentieth centuries shows this already to have been the case, that is even in trades which, and at a time when, Weber's minimum transfer cost theories were reckoned most applicable. What is more, it is clear that some entrepreneurs realized this well enough. An early Victorian writer on the iron trade put it as follows in a chapter full of perception and wisdom entitled 'On the employment of capital in ironworks and colleries':

There are two main causes of want of success in establishing profitable ironworks: the one, injudicious selection of sites, as affecting carriage, and quality of minerals, royalty etc.; the other, want of judgement in carrying out works even when the situation, quality of coal and other minerals, facilities of carriage, and arrangements as to royalties etc. are of favourable character (Wilkie 1857).

In fact, efficiency in processing could do much to cancel out the cost disadvantage of a poor location, for, as it was put ninety years after Wilkie, high economic efficiency thereby compensated for low 'geonomic efficiency' (Renner 1947).

Locational choice and transfer costs

The questions of locational choice which bother major industrial concerns today—if and when they are able to break away from economic, social, and political constraints and so do more than merely extend existing works—are national in scope: it is important to recognize that this was not commonly the case 150 or even 100 years ago. At that stage heavy industries were often located with regional procurement of materials and regional demand in mind; in this second respect at least they were like most service trades today. With Britain as the workshop of the world they commonly moved on from regional to overseas supply as easily as they marketed interregionally within Britain. Thus shipyards which in the golden heyday of British shipbuilding in the generation before World War I supplied the merchant marines of the whole world began by constructing colliers to undertake deliveries from local pits. The alkali works which were rapidly built up along south Tyneside from Salt Meadows, Gateshead, to Jarrow Slake in the 1830s and 1840s were designed first to supply soap- and glassworks in the Ouseburn on the eastern edge of Newcastle or in South Shields, and only after that gained a national and international market. Even so, with new, easy, and fairly low-cost bulk transport the cheaper producer, or a plant with high- or special-quality products or rapidly expanding capacity pushing beyond the ability of merely regional outlets, was soon involved in major inter-regional movements of heavy industrial goods. One example was the deluge of Scotch iron which ruined ironworks and caused riots of the unemployed in South Wales or the Black Country in the 1840s, induced troubled Tyneside ironmasters to go so far as to acquire blackband ore royalties in central Scotland but was followed within a few years of the opening of the Cleveland main seam in 1850 by a massive return flow of Teesside iron. By 1867 it was reckoned that Cleveland iron ore cost less than one-quarter as much as that of Scotland, and though the iron was inferior it was used widely, mixed with Scotch iron. In 1867 70 000 tons of Middlesbrough pig iron was delivered to Scotland. Shipped into Grangemouth it went from there either to the foundries of the Falkirk district or inland via the Forth and Clyde Canal to the foundries of the Maryhill district of Glasgow or the malleable ironworks around Motherwell (*Colliery Guardian* 1868).

Elsewhere, the growth of good communications had other effects. Once, as a Black Country man remarked in 1861, the Staffordshire iron trade had been able to pay high prices for its minerals, 'but now, in consequence of railway communication, when we have all the world to compete with, and when coal is delivered in this district from north, east, south and west, and at nearly the same prices we are paying for getting, it is indeed time for us to bestir ourselves if we are to exist and compete with other districts' (Bailey 1861).

The transport charges which determine the economic value of place are by no means simple. With very large overheads in relation to their movement costs, coastal shipping, canals, and above all railways have a great deal of freedom in the rates which they fix, rates giving total revenue which as far as possible covers total costs but which in relation to each type of goods may vary widely according to the time-honoured principle of charging what the traffic will bear so long as that freight rate at least covers the movement cost of the goods and makes some contribution to the overheads of the whole system. Moreover, it is important to recognize that because of their exceptional size and complexity transport concerns have been the very epitome of 'bounded rationality' as is clear in the study of the routes which were chosen for railways—their overbuilding and regional rivalries—or in the keen competition between too many ports, not one of which was prepared to abandon its pretensions. The structure and irrationalities of transport systems provide the environment of spatial costing within which manufacturing industries make their own locational decisions.

The grouping and tapering of freight rates, ballast rates, the whole complicated field of special rates, break-of-bulk-point advantages—all these affected industrial locations. Ballast rates by collier returning to the Tyne constituted one of the main advantages, along with cheap small coal, of the Tyneside Leblanc alkali industry into the 1860s. The other major seat of the industry was Merseyside, where salt from the Northwich-Winsford area could be cheaply delivered to the works of St. Helens, Widnes, and Runcorn by river and canal. Tyneside also used Cheshire salt, mostly carried by canal and then via the Trent to Humber ports where it was picked up by colliers returning north and carried at a nominal charge to the Tyne. This reduced the cost of salt, but even so in 1860–1 it was still twice as expensive as in Lancashire works. In the final stages of alkali manufacture limestone was employed. The Merseyside works obtained this in part from North Wales but mainly from the early ancestors of the giant quaries which I.C.I. still operates in the neighbourhood of Buxton. Tyneside's limestone cost less than one-quarter as much for it again came at ballast rates, chalk being dredged from the Thames mainly at Greenhithe and Northfleet or even brought in colliers returning from making deliveries to Paris—the so-called 'French Cliff' from the Seine. Unfortunately for the alkali trade the development of the screw steamer, built of iron and with a double bottom, gradually changed ballasting systems, water being let in as the steamer passed down the Thames and pumped out as it approached the coal staithes of the Tyne for its next cargo. Improved efficiency of operation, a technical edge in a basic industry, in this instance seriously injured the competitive powers of another (Gossage 1861; Richardson and Watts 1863; Armstrong 1864).

It was always regarded as an advantage to a heavy industrial district to have competing means of transport either through different media or through different companies. Throughout the late nineteenth century Black Country iron- and metalworking firms constantly complained that they were unfairly treated in the question of railway rates compared with other districts. In Cleveland, for instance, even though the North Eastern Railway came to control the whole district, the possibility of shipping by sea was always a moderating influence on the level at which freight rates could be set. Moreover, few of the Staffordshire firms were big enough to stand up to the railway companies and they were so numerous that the railways could view the elimination of many with equanamity. Finally, although the West Midlands was served by three great systems, the London and North Western, the Midland, and the Great Western, the companies had bound themselves by the concordat in 1861 not to grant any concession rates. There were similar examples of collusion elsewhere, for instance in the Sheffield area or in south Lancashire (Warren 1970; *Depression of trade and industry* 1886; *Railway Agreements and Amalgamations* 1911). It is noteworthy that a freight-rate policy which speeded the decline of the mineral-based heavy industries of south Staffordshire thereby also hastened the incoming of new, further-processing metal industries which laid the foundation for the economic dynamism of the West Midlands in the twentieth century. No major coal or ironmaking district declined so decisively as the West Midlands: the outcome, helped on by other favourable factors, notably an early metalworking diversity and a central location, was a new role for the region in the national economy.

Elsewhere railway freight-rate policies sometimes helped to preserve old location patterns. Until the early 1960s a row of antiquated blast furnaces towered above the lowlands of the Wreake Valley at Asfordby near Melton Mowbray in Leicestershire. These were the landscape evidence of a process of industrial evolution which began in 1881 when the first furnaces came into production to work up iron ore which the Holwell Iron Company had previously supplied to Derbyshire iron firms which now had integrated backward to control their own ore supplies. In 1902 another step in forward integration took Holwell into iron founding and particularly cast iron pipe manufacture in direct competition with the bigger Derbyshire firms. By 1907 Holwell was capable of producing some 120 000 tons of pig iron annually, but it operated in an isolated location which was served by a single railway company, the Midland. In 1909 the Holwell Iron Company appealed to the Railway and Canal Commissioners against Midland rebates to the Stavely and Stanton companies amounting to 1d. and 2d. per mile respectively. The Commissioners upheld the rebates, not because the Derbyshire firms were bigger and so provided more traffic than Holwell, but because, if the Midland had not granted them it would have lost traffic to rivals for their business. At a time when use of low-grade ore and fuel economy were tending to favour orefield ironmaking locations such a pricing policy helped to preserve the old coalfield—and formerly also Coal Measure iron ore—locations and to limit Holwell's growth (*Railway Rates Tribunal* 1911, pp. 393–5; I.C.T.R. 1907).

In other instances, railway competition and company size together gave lower rates for one location and considerably higher rates for a competitive location in the same region. A notable South Wales case came to a head in 1887–8. A number of works on the northern outcrop of the coalfield had struggled to adjust to changing sources of minerals, particularly the movement from local ore—the so called Welsh 'mine'— to imported, richer ore, and had also rebuilt their works to enable them to produce steel rather than finished iron. In the process of these changes there had already been an enormous shut-down of works throughout South Wales—'Llwydcoed is a ruin, Gadlys a wreck, Treforest rusting to decay, Abernant more forlorn than Nineveh, Hirwain more desolate than the Cities of the Plain' as a trade journal put it with a distinctive analgam of Victorian journalese, classical education, and biblical imagery (I.C.T.R. 1886). Two of the firms which had made the change, but were to fail within the next few years and transfer their energies from iron and steel to coal, were the Rhymney and Tredegar companies. The Rhymney Iron Company complained in 1888 about the freight rates charged by the Rhymney Railway Company on its minerals and on finished products as compared with the rates charged by the railway company to the Dowlais Iron Company. The case revealed the role of the varying range of movement costs, the effects of railway company competition, and the significance of the size of traffice (Table 2). In

TABLE 2

Freight charges per ton to Phymney Iron Company and Dowlais Iron Company 1888   (New Pence)

| | Nominal rates to | | Alleged rebates to Dowlais Iron |
	Rhymney Iron	Dowlais Iron	
Iron ore from Cardiff[1]	8·5	9·5	2·5
Coal from pits to Cardiff	7·5	8·5	1·5
Iron and steel to Cardiff	8·5	9·5	2·5

[1] The rail distances to Bute Docks, Cardiff, was 24 miles from Rhymney and 24½ miles from Dowlais.

Based on: Iron and Coal Trades Review, 27 July 1888, 132.

reply to the complaint the Rhymney Railway Company noted, firstly, that it undertook much more marshalling at both ends of the journey for Rhymney than for Dowlais. Secondly, Dowlais was much the bigger firm and therefore not only provided more traffic but also had more bargaining power with the railway company. In 1887 Rhymney Railway Company carried 52 000 tons of iron ore for Rhymney Iron and 260 000 tons for Dowlais, and altogether the latter provided it with three times as much traffic as its rival. Finally, Rhymney had only the Rhymney Railway for traffic to and from the coast whereas Dowlais could also ship through Merthyr Tydfil via the Taff Vale or by a more roundabout route out of the region by the London and North Western Line (I.C.T.R. 1887, 1888 (1) and (2)).

Generally, once established, heavy industries with their large fixed investment were immovable, and hence to that further degree at the mercy of railway companies. It is true that there were some notable cases when, partly at least in response to high rail-freight charges, firms either built a new coastal works as Dowlais Iron did at Cardiff in 1890 or moved wholly to the coast as with the outstanding movement of Cammell's rail business from Dronfield, south of Sheffield, to Workington in 1882, the transfer of Nettlefolds from Shropshire to South Wales in 1885, and, in the first years of the twentieth century, the removal of iron- and steelmaking from Spennymoor, County Durham, to the new works at Cargo Fleet on the Tees estuary. In the years 1898 to 1912 rail-freight charges were a central consideration in the migration of a number of Black Country firms to the coast (Warren 1970). Not only were differential freight charges a significant factor in interplant rivalry within Britain, but the general high level of these charges—itself a product of various factors including the early construction of the system, the generally short hauls, and probably also unimaginative railway pricing policies—penalized British heavy industry in international competition, that is, played a part in evolving world location patterns. There is little doubt of this, even though the heavy industries not infrequently exaggerated the rail-freight issue, for it shifted the blame for Britain falling behind on to other shoulders. An example is the iron trade report on continental competition in 1896 (B.I.T.A. 1896 (1) and (2)). A few years later Carnegie remarked that one of the first steps to a new international competitiveness for Britain's industry should be to make a bonfire of her rolling stock (Jeans 1902).

Process cost differences

A poor location in terms of movement costs may be redeemed by low process costs, the result of either localized advantages or high efficiency. The last point is significant, for whereas some low costs are due to natural advantages, more are probably the result of human effort of response to a challenge, often of an intrinsically poor location.

In the past when new resources were being opened up in the British mineral fields and there were many more smaller firms and plants, process costs and profit margins almost certainly varied much more than today. By summer 1853, three years after the Main Seam was discovered, Cleveland iron was costing only 27s. a ton to make when the price was about 60s. Production costs were about half those in some other districts (*Mining Journal* 1853). Interesting light is thrown on the matter of process cost variation by the situation in the works of the United Alkali Company formed in autumn 1890 to include almost all the Leblanc Alkali works in Britain, 48 in all (U.A.C. 1890).

In the next few years U.A.C. closed many works in order to rationalize its operations but in the second half of the 1890s there still remained substantial differences. To some extent these reflected the already complex nature of the heavy chemical industry and its technology so that a main product in one works was a joint product or even a by-product in another, but even in the same localities the production cost differences which U.A.C. accountants revealed were most striking.

In the case of the U.A.C. plants it is not wholly clear what the cause of production cost differences were but it seems probable that they resulted from differences in the efficiency of machinery or even in the degree of mechanization itself. In other instances, there is no doubt that interregional differences in wages were important. As noted earlier, South Wales was greatly troubled by the competition of Scottish ironworks in the 1840s. Whereas Staffordshire firms reacted to the same challenge by concentration on higher-value products, Welsh works cut their costs by debasing their quality. They used much scoria or forge cinder in their furnaces which often produced a very inferior iron and also, strictly in breach of contract for their rails, used a good deal of imported Scotch pig iron in puddling (Bruce 1853; Grunner and Lan 1861 and 1863). Much of this material went to cheap United States railroad construction; a few years later Hewitt reported ' . . . in my visits to those gigantic establishments which have grown up in the mountains of South Wales it was humiliating to find that the vilest trash which could be dignified by the name of iron went universally by the name of the American rail' (Hewitt 1868, 10—11).

South Wales had other process cost advantages. One, which helped them in the competition with Teesside, particularly when the basic Bessemer process seemed likely to allow the latter to become a major producer of steel rail from Cleveland ore, was the availablity of coal not not only from nearer mines but also from mines owned to a greater extent than in the North East by the ironmasters. Another substantial advantage was lower-cost labour, presumably a product of both the earlier development of the South Wales minerals and metal centres and the absence of major alternative outlets for labour there (*Colliery Guardian* 1879). Indeed there seems to have been a marked behavioural basis for the lower wages of the South Wales district, a strong reluctance of the workers to move away from the district. As summed up in a review of the trade in 1881

The cheapness of labour in South Wales is always a factor in the consideration of the production of iron and steel, and while matters remain in that condition it has a manifest advantage over the North of England, where only those Welsh ironworkers go who have been compelled, through the closing of works in their own district, to seek other employment (*Iron* 1882).

Another process cost factor was scale of plant. This, as considered above, was clearly an advantage when dealing with locational disadvantages but at a time when management skills were less reliable than later there were scale diseconomies as well, notably a lack of flexibility and of adaptability. Hewitt in his 1868 Report from the Paris Exposition recognized the organizational problem well enough, and indeed, interestingly, was overwhelmed by the size of some British works which still exceeded the American norm. He wrote particularly of five works which produced over 100 000 tons of iron or steel annually, John Browns in Sheffield, Bolckow and Vaughan on Teesside, the Barrow Hematite Iron and Steel Company, and, in South Wales, Dowlais, and Ebbw Vale.

Large towns are required to house the workmen and their families, hundreds of miles of rails and thousands of cars are appropriated to their special use. The human mind is lost in wonder at the combination of material and intellectual elements required for the organization and conduct of such gigantic operations . . . (Hewitt 1868, 29).

Shortly before, and for a few years after, the death of Sir John Guest Dowlais was the biggest plant in Britain but it worked at a heavy loss (Bessborough 1950). In 1857 William Menelaus, later one of Britain's most renowned iron- and steelmasters, submitted a report on the plant to the chief engineer. The average fuel consumption was higher than that of well-managed furnaces in the district and whereas in recent years nearly every Welsh works had made great strides in the yields of the furnace and in producing cheaper iron their own quality was very irregular and inferior, in fact 'Dowlais was standing still; instead of taking the lead as from her size and position she ought, she was quietly falling into the rear'. Moreover, operations were ill balanced, forge and mill power being far too small in relation to the capacity of the blast furnaces (Menelaus 1857).

Bounded rationality and the 'satisficer' principle in location

In an era when 'economic man' was commonly regarded as the business ideal and when the iron law of wages seemed to have an inflexible grip on the relationships between employers and their work force it is quite clear that partial knowledge, irrational decision-taking, and less than rigidly economic business were common. The result was the choice or maintenance of suboptimal locations and the use of processes or of factor inputs that were far from the ideal. Poor locations in turn brought out qualities of management which might not have been necessary in better conditions.

Partial knowledge has two aspects: ignorance as to resources or technology or a conceptual framework which leads to erroneous expectations. The most obvious example of the first was when a plant was located in ignorance of resources which later greatly improved, or relatively worsened its situation. The development of the Billingham-Port Clarence section of Teesside provides an outstanding example. When Bell brothers began to build the Port Clarence Ironworks in 1852 they did not know of the great salt deposits beneath it, which made them important producers in the 1880s and 1890s and for a few years of some significance in alkali too. A mile away Brunner and Mond appear to have been similarly ignorant of the anhydrite which underlay the major sulphate of ammonia plant which they were building at Billingham in the early 1920s. Every time a new mineral district was opened the techniques applied were the best known elsewhere, and only later were great advances made as each district modified both equipment and practice to take full advantage of the peculiarities of local materials. Thus Cleveland ironmasters built Staffordshire-type furnaces before they realized that the type of ore and above all the superb Durham coke would permit them to operate much taller ones. By the mid-1860s they were pioneering new high levels of furnace efficiency and practice including developments in fuel economy, which gave them over-all levels of coal consumption per ton of pig iron only-two-thirds those of Staffordshire (Cowper 1865; Bauerman 1874). In short, as knowledge increased so also the Cleveland ironmasters responded to the challenge of their greater distance from coal supplies by emphasizing fuel economy,

first through bigger furnaces, then with better blast heating—the introduction of the regenerative stove—and further still in heat conservation
in steelmaking as with the introduction of the soaking pits by Gjers in
1881. The Scots tried to follow the Cleveland lead but their splint coal
would not support the same high blast furnace column as Durham coke,
and those who experimented frequently had to lower their stacks again.
Another factor was the general exhaustion of Scottish iniative in ironmaking. Only thirty years after Scotch iron had been the scourge of
ironmasters and men in southern Britain a Scot had to admit 'There is
little of a novel or advanced kind, with an exception here and there, to
be found in the smelting practice of the Scottish iron-masters' (Day
1876). In the Lincolnshire district it took ironmasters some time to
realize the potentialities of their limy ores so that, in accordance with
normal practice, limestone was quarried, carried, and used as flux before
it was realized that the practice was not only unnecessary but actually
harmful!

The conceptual framework within which partial knowledge of resources and techniques operated led the heavy trades to continue to
think along old lines even where or when this was quite inappropriate.
In South Wales coal, Coal Measure ironstone and iron production seemed
to go together, and so in the early 1860s when commentators began to
recognize that Rhondda coal would be a formidable competitor for the
Aberdare Valley the whole economic growth process was believed to be
only in its infancy for ' . . . as yet there has been no ironwork established'
(*Colliery Guardian* 1863). In 1828 the last Wealden furnace at
Ashburnham near Battle was blown out, but for one hundred years the
possibility of reviving the Kentish section intrigued commentators time
and again. In the latter half of the nineteenth century it was envisaged
that North East coast and Welsh coal or coke would be used there
(Society of Arts 1860; Bauerman 1874 (2)). By the early twentieth
century the opening of the Kent coalfield and initial impressions that
the coal made an excellent coke led to a flood of suggestions and even
proposals for iron- and steelmaking. Steel industry representatives
referred to ideal assembly conditions there and anticipated a 'big steel
industry' (Hamilton 1920; Samuelson 1922). Carried away by the
thinking of industry spokesmen the pioneer regional planners of the
twenties not unnaturally anticipated the classical, apparently automatic
coal-iron-metal industries growth spiral—'with coal and iron on the spot,
blast furnaces and steel works established, other economic minerals
obtainable and electric power in almost unlimited quantities available it
is inconceivable but that many other industries will find their way into

East Kent' (Abercrombie and Archibold 1923). Even though the model proved inapplicable to Kent its persistence for so long perhaps helps to account for the failure of the steel trade to follow the new planning which Ford's Dagenham furnaces, based upon water-borne distant material supplies and a local market, pointed to a few years later. Thameside's tremendous development prospects for steel were never subsequently to be taken up.

Partial knowledge clearly helps to explain irrational decision-taking but the very word 'rational' assumes a norm which does not in fact exist, for such a norm would presume universal acceptance of the same criteria for success in business operations. In many instances we do not know enough to decide whether an apparently suboptimal location choice reflected ignorance or a less than fully economic motivation. In the 1870s John Brown retired from the famous Sheffield firm he had built up from spring and special steelmaking into a major rail, railway equipment, and armour plate operation, and decided to enter shipbuilding. Whether it was because of close knowledge of a nearby centre or failure to realize its limited potential as opposed to the bigger shipbuilding rivers he chose to invest in Earles Shipbuilding Company in Hull. When, a quarter of a century later, John Brown and Co. decided it was opportune to extend into shipbuilding they chose Clydebank with the whole tradition of Scottish shipbuilding behind it. Through another seventy-five years of illustrious shipbuilding history this choice proved to have higher survival value than Sir John's. The Earle's yard was dismantled by National Shipbuilders Security Ltd. in 1932–3.

For business, or perhaps partly for social reasons, a firm may struggle on in a location which has a low survival value. By initiative it may even do well there. North East England contains two outstanding examples in the steelworks at Hartlepool and Consett which just before nationalization made 8 per cent of Britain's steel. Hartlepool was initially an ill-located works well away from both Durham coking coal and Cleveland ore. In the 1870s when better located finished iron works failed it went over into steelmaking. In the mergers and rationalization of the early twentieth century it became the nucleus of the South Durham group, and between the wars began also to produce large diameter pipes made from plate. The persistence and irrationality of the Talbot family which ran it carried South Durham through the successive post-1945 development plans of the British steel industry in which it was initially scheduled for early closure. Boosted in the fifties by the worldwide demand for large diameter pipe for oil and gas carriage, South Durham prospered by virtue of its product specialization rather than its location. In 1959 it began work on major new plant in which it failed to install the new oxygen steel processes which others regarded as proved. Within twelve years of 1961 inauguration of this new works the British Steel Corporation had announced that in the process of rationalization the Hartlepool complex would be closed by the early 1980s with the whole of steel-making concentrated on South Teesside near the new ore docks (Heal 1974; Warren 1969). The development and maintenance of Consett works is too complex to examine here but it has involved 125 years of struggle to maintain a location of inferior value from the time when the Cleveland Main Seam was discovered in the summer of 1850. Outstanding managers and directors, pioneering in products and processes, maintenance of high efficiency, freight-rate concessions from the North Eastern Railway Company, and profit transfers from coal and coke sales to the iron- and steelmaking account were important at various times in maintaining its viability.

In South Wales the situation was not dissimilar and here contrasts in business efficiency and motivation were more clear cut. Some works were sure that profitability was all-important. At the beginning of the twentieth century one of the leading rail producers is said to have remarked 'We do not conduct our works for philanthropic reasons, and when we cease to pay we close down' (*Engineer* 1903). Over half a century before, at the time of the renewal of the Dowlais lease, the owner Lord Bute replied to a memorial from the town of Dowlais that he did not consider that the neighbourhood had any claims on him, but Guest and his wife were convinced of their social responsibilities—'The responsibilities are so great in a moral as well as a pecuniary point of view' wrote Lady Guest just after the renewal; a little later she was still convinced, though rather less emphatic. It was, she noted in her diary, Guest's duty ' . . . to incur toil and risk for the population he has encouraged there, as long as he can do it without actual detriment to his family' (Bessborough, 1950).

In other cases works were kept going either because of ignorance of the true cost situation—a not uncommon dilemma in the mid-nineteenth century, when primitive accounting would not always distinguish between revenue from coal sales and those from iron—or for compassionate reasons. When the Aberdare Iron Company failed in 1875 it was reckoned that investigation would show that there had been no really profitable results for a quarter of a century (*Iron* 1875). The progress of Cyfarthfa illustrates the behavioural factor in iron and steel very well.

The Cyfarthfa works dated from 1765, seven years later than Dowlais. Richard Crawshay who came some twenty years later from Normanton,

Yorkshire, to manage it was a man of strong will, no sentiment, and a born ruler of men (Wilkins 1903). The quality of the Crawshay 'dynasty' seems to have been as important as the mineral endowment of the area in pushing Cyfarthfa to a pre-eminent position in the Welsh iron trade (Addis 1957). Richard's grandson, William Crawshay was, as Charlotte Guest put it in her charcterization of the rivals of Dowlais, 'beyond all rule and description and quite one of those meteoric beings whom it is quite impossible to account for' (Bessborough 1950)—in return for which Crawshay rather ungraciously personalized Dowlais as 'the devil'. In Cyfarthfa Castle, built specially for the Crawshays, William seems to have suffered illusions of grandeur but he made every effort to maintain his works in a high degree of perfection. Strangely he would not follow Guest in sending out agents to canvass orders for rails but he was prepared to stock bar iron in bad times in order to keep the works in operation. By 1860 Crawshay was convinced of the difficulty of competing with other iron districts on the basis of Welsh ore—this 'miserable patch of lean argillaceous mine' as he put it. In 1860 he wrote to his son 'I really think it would be wise to give up the iron trade entirely and sell the coal' (Morris and Williams 1958), but two years later he was still ready to struggle on. 'I do not see any way very clear for the Welsh iron trade for the future'. 'Those cheap ores in the Cleveland district, Cumberland and Northampton are making awfully cheap iron . . . working in Wales on 20s. ore in opposition to 3s., 3s. 6d. and 7s. even will be a very uphill game' (Addis 1957, 132). Yet at this time, as two French metallurgists found, Cyfarthfa was 'in excellent condition, contrasting with the dilapidated and disordered appearance of many of the Welsh works' (Grunner and Lan 1863, 134). Cyfarthfa was closed down from April 1874 to October 1879—a closure which began with a strike over a refusal to accept a wage reduction which was double that which other Welsh ironmasters were demanding but which continued for more than four years after the strike was settled. Cyfarthfa's subsequent history showed that a major location could too easily be perpetuated beyond its reasonable term. Reopened in 1879 to continue the manufacture of iron rails, the plant was wholly dismantled in 1882, the ironworks rebuilt, and a 'magnificant steelworks laid down'. Cyfarthfa's revival brought new life to Merthyr but the works seem to have been burdened by unbalanced operations—the cogging and rail mill had capacity to roll double the quantity of rails the works started with (*Iron* 1884). By 1895 only 'the exceptional excellence of the management' was said to have preserved it from the catastrophe which had fallen on Rhymney and Tredegar (*Engineer* 1895), but in 1890 it had to be turned into a limited company and in March

1902 went through the ultimate humiliation when its share capital was acquired by Guest, Keen and Company. Closed before World War I, reactivated in the war, it was afterwards out of work and was gradually dismantled. Cyfarthfa's locational deficiencies had not prevented it from at least sixty years of operations of very questionable viability. The model which it represented from the Victorian and Edwardian world was unfortunately also to be taken up and followed by firms and planners over the next half-century.

European steelmakers have in recent years been accused of a so-called 'forgemaster' attitude, a technical rather than a commercial interest in their operations, essentially a philosophy of 'we're in business because we like making steel'. (The converse rational accountant's attitude was long ago summed up with admirable directness by Harry Brearley the Yorkshire pioneer of stainless steels as 'we're not here to make steel but to make brass'.) To the extent that technical interest for its own sake was given precedence over cost minimization—and clearly it was by no means always opposed to it in the long run—opportunities were given to those who chose to operate on more strictly economic principles. In each of the major British metallurgical districts this led to the emergence of new companies to compete with, displace, and eventually often absorb the older, more traditional concerns, as with Colvilles in Scotland, Dorman Long in the north east, and Baldwins, Richard Thomas, and Guest, Keen in Wales. The arrival of the new dominant concerns was assisted by the movement fron iron to steel. Similarly, in heavy chemicals the dominance of Brunner and Mond marked the progress of the Solvay process at the expense of the Leblanc concerns. Here also the impact— locational as well as commercial, as Northwhich and its Cheshire satellites displaced the old alkali towns—of new aggressive business methods was of great importance. Ludwig Mond was ruthless with himself and de- manded the same standards of others. John Brunner highlighted the issue in a speech made at a prize-giving for students of Northwich science and art classes in 1896. Trade in Britain was, he said, mostly managed by people who knew little about it.

The number of great businesses that were in the hands of men who cared more about fox hunting, shooting or fishing than about their business was very long. If one looked round it seemed that it was the ambition of well-to-do people in this country to bring their people up not to business but to sport. He would assure every student that there was a great deal of prosperity, an open road to fortune, to everyone who studied a trade so as to know more about it than his neighbour (*Chemical Trade Journal* 1896).

To the extent that Brunner's assertion of the generality of this attitude was true of British business it had a locational significance much wider than that of the contrasts between Northwich and Widnes. As with the deficiencies in British rail transport it contributed to the decline in the international standing of British manufacturing: the significance of the new British business ethos extended to worldwide locational patterns.

The broad trends in locational values reflect alterations in the composition of material imputs and outputs and are also considerably affected by technological change. The discovery of Lanarkshire Blackband, Cleveland and Jurassic belt ore, or Teesside salt, the inventions of Cort, Neilson, Bessemer, or Thomas, Solvay's process or the progress of iron and later of steel shipbilding—all of these undoubtedly changed the broad patterns of locational forces and they alone represent such a comglomeration of elements, of 'noise' in the locational models as to seriously limit the latter's application in the real world. Behavioural factors constitute an even bigger permissive element in locational change. Britain's heavy industry, so early in the race, conducted in a large number of units and widely throughout the country, and with management which, perhaps by national origins and certainly by education and social training is not coldly logical, provides a rich field for the study of locations affected by non-economic motivation. Here the behavioural factor ceases to be a troublesome noise obscuring the majestic main themes of locational change and comes into the forefront of the composition.

3 Factor mobility, technical change, and regional economic growth

From an early stage of British industrialization the factors of production proved highly mobile. Roebuck, the Birmingham inventor of the lead chamber process of sulphuric acid production, built his first works at Prestonpans in 1749. Eleven years later, across the Firth of Forth, the first Carron blast furnace was lit, a decisive step in the industrialization of Scotland undertaken by a group, one of whose leaders was Garbett of Birmingham and which involved English entrepreneurship, capital, and skilled labour. Capital and managerial talent for the rapid growth of South Wales ironmaking late in the eighteenth century also came from England—Guest from Broseley, Shropshire, Crawshay from the West Riding. As Shropshire ironmaking declined in the nineteenth century the Darby family moved to positions of pre-eminence in both North and South Wales, at Brymbo and at Ebbw Vale. In the mid-nineteenth century the growth of a completely new mineral and metal district such as Cleveland had to be supplied with factors of production from outside. They came from Tyneside, the West Riding, Liverpool and South Lancashire, and from older metal districts. John Vaughan, the technical partner of the Teesside pioneers Bolckow and Vaughan, came from Dowlais via Carlisle and Walker on Tyne; Bolckow, his commercial associate from Mecklenburg, through the grain business of the Tyne. Samuelson, who also played a significant role in Teesside development, was already in agricultural engineering in Banbury. There was a flood of Welsh management to the North East, Richards from Dowlais to Bolckow's, Jenkins from Dowlais to Consett (*Colliery Guardian* 1882). The case of Edward Williams is of especial interest for it illustrates both the technical interplay between districts and the way in which talented managers who later moved on to invest their savings in ownership could thereby help to preserve indifferent plants. Born in Merthyr, Williams worked in various posts in Dowlais works from 1842 to 1864. In 1865 be became General Manager at Eston. In 1871, while holding this post, with Menelaus of Dowlais and others he purchased the Forest furnaces at Pontypridd and the Tredegar Iron Works, both of which were remodelled. He resigned from Bolckow and Vaughan in 1876 but three years later purchased the Linthorpe blast furnace in Middlesbrough. His final great enterprise brought him back to South Wales to design the Cyfarthfa steelworks (Civil Engineers 1887). The mobility of managerial and technical talent was not only interregional but also international. Bolckow was a prominent example for the iron trade. The alkali trade provides three very important ones: George Lunge who worked on Tyneside, Ferdinand Hurter who, from working for a Widnes firm, became the first reseach director of United Alkali, and, outstandingly, Ludwig Mond, from Cassel district who more than any other man after the original inventor made Solvay's process not only a technical but above all a commercial success (see also Erickson 1959).

Both unskilled and skilled labour also moved widely. A good deal of the early labour in the furnaces of the Scunthorpe district was from the Black County and, very much in accordance with Staffordshire mores, there are stories of men deserting the furnaces to chase rabbits in the sandy ground which overlies the Frodingham ironstone bed. Irishmen were always an important source of unskilled labour in new heavy districts. In the 1830s they were busy fighting the Welsh and English in the coal and iron towns of South Wales; in 1873 there were 400 of them employed on the Port Clarence blast furnaces (*Colliery Guardian* 1873). Much of the early puddling in central Scotland's new malleable iron-works in the late 1830s and the 1840s was done by men specially brought in from the Midlands and Wales, and until at least the end of the 1950s a row of brick-built houses at Calderbank at the head of the Monkland Canal stood as a landscape expression of this, housing built specially for immigrant Sassenach workers, a great improvement on the stone hovels in which the indigenous labourers were forced to live.

A further aspect of mobility involved the investment of profits. A large proportion of these were ploughed back into works extension, but, as indicated above, a good deal were transferred from one district to another. Some even went overseas. In the mid-1870s and at a critical time in the fortunes of the finished iron trade of the North East coast the Southern States Coal, Iron and Land Company was launched to invest Teesside capital in the Southern Appalachian mineral districts of the U.S.A. The principal directors were Thomas Whitwell of Thornaby Iron Works, E. L. Pease, an ex-mayor of Darlington, and H. F. Pease of the Middlesborough Chemical Works (*Engineer* 1876). When profits were invested, not in further manufacturing but in land or property, there was a marked emphasis on the south of Britain: in short, from coal and iron districts there was taking place that transfer of wealth which was helping to lay the foundation of a classical 'north-south' problem for the twentieth century. It is true that there were exceptions to this south-ward orientation. Lord Armstrong, having built his Germanic-type retreat of Cragside near Rothbury, later bought and restored the ancient castle of Bamburgh. On the other hand, Guest of Dowlais not only entered Parliament byt also acquired Wimbourne estate in Dorset, and his Merthyr business neighbour William Crawshay retired from the horrors of Cyfarthfa to the delights of the greenhouses on his properties in Caversham near Reading. Charles Cammell, who had originally arrived in Sheffield with £5 in his pocket, built up not only great works in the Don Valley and at Penistone but also properties which represented a gradual move away from the district in which his money was made. He first lived in Clarkehouse Road, then in Loxley House, and in 1857 moved to Norton Hall between Sheffield and Dronfield and took every opportunity to buy up property there. He also owned a 2000 acre Hampshire estate (Stainton 1924).

The geography of innovation and technical change

Change of technology will probably substitute wholly new raw materials for old, may affect the type of production and the tonnage and the kind of by- or joint product. It will therefore alter material balances. The change will probably also affect the scale, capitalization, and labour needs of the operation. For all these reasons it will influence locational values. Technical changes sometimes take the form of very small steps, as with the continuous progress in fuel economy in iron smelting or puddling, or reduction in the amount of coal used in the black ash furnaces of the Leblanc trade. Sometimes, however, it represents a much bigger departure from conventional practices and in fewer cases its effects may fairly be described as revolutionary. Examples of the last were the hot blast, Solvay's ammonia-soda process, the Bessemer and basic Bessemer converters, or the arrival in interwar Britain of the hot strip mill.

The invention which is the initiator of technical change sometimes comes from within the industry, but frequently in the nineteenth century, when individual inventive genius was still more important than the collective results of large research teams working in industrial laboratories, it came from outside, from workers who were aware of the bottlenecks and the opportunities in the heavy industries but were not engaged in them. This was certainly the case with the major innovations in the iron and steel trades. The hot blast which unlocked the genii of Lanarkshire blackband ore and splint coal came from Neilson, who was working in a Glasgow gasworks, Henry Bessemer was an established and highly versatile free-lance inventor, and Sidney Gilchrist Thomas, a poor, pale-faced magistrate's clerk. In each case they succeeded in achieving what those within the industry had failed to do—I. L. Bell had spent some £45 000 in futile attempts to make steel from Cleveland pig iron (J.S.C.I. 1905).

By the mid-nineteenth century a highly developed technical Press and the existence of learned or professional societies and of the telegraph and railway ensured that knowledge of inventions was spread almost instantaneously. When E. W. Richards was testing the Thomas process at Eston in 1879 Middlesbrough was 'besieged' as contemporary writers put it, by representatives of continental iron firms. Adoption rather than initial interest in inventions was affected by a variety of factors. One was the suitability of resources and scales of production. Scottish ironmasters took an early interest in Bessemer's process but the unsuitability of Scottish ores and irons for acid steelmaking and still more their continuing success in old lines of business prevented them from going into Bessemer steelmaking on a big scale. Cleveland, emminently successful with its wrought iron trade until after the Franco-Prussian War, was not receptive to steelmaking until this trade collapsed. Most Black Country firms were ruled out because their ore was too phosphoric, their plants too small, and their operations too disintegrated. Enterprise or openness to new ideas was also an important factor and old districts were not receptive. An early and vicious attack on Bessemer was led by Joseph Hall of Tipton, who had been a pioneer in wrought iron innovations thirty years earlier (Hall 1857). Sheffield, booming with railway business and full of men of drive like John Brown, Charles Cammell, and their lieutenants was a natural first home of Bessemer's process.

Innovations not only built up and extended industrial districts but also brought down those areas which for material or human reasons did not adopt them. In the mid-1880s Walter Weldon noted the destruction which the advance of the Solvay process was creating in the old Leblanc alkali centres but, being imbued with Victorian values, he was compelled to accept, albeit regretfully, 'By such changes individuals may and alas! do suffer, but the world gains by them' (Weldon 1884). A few years before an outstanding railway contractor noted 'The discoveries of science are frequently afforded with ruinous consequences to large masses of workmen' (Brassey 1879). The case to which he referred was the collapse of the wrought iron trade as a result of chronic depression and the simultaneous advance of Bessemer steel into fields where the iron trade had been dominant. Of 45 000 puddlers formerly at work in northern England and Wales less than half were still at work when he wrote.

In the West Midlands in particular many wrought iron firms survived for many years by switching to finished lines in which iron was still regarded as superior to steel; now and later many of them also made the successful transfer from making and rolling their own wrought iron into rolling purchased steel, they became rerollers, a considerably number of which have survived in the West Midlands to the present day. In South Wales and the North East the product range of finished iron works was narrower. They had dominated the business in wrought iron rails and in the North in particular it had grown rapidly as a result. The North East had 404 puddling furnaces in 1860, 2153 by 1875, but by 1884, after a short-lived boom in wrought iron shipbuilding material, only 843. Many works which went out of production then were not revived or replaced and a few communities settled down into a long-drawn-out decline. Witton Park, west of Bishop Auckland, developed as an ironworks location in 1846, was being described as 'a conscript of Durham villages' little more than forty years later and has since then had ninety years of shrinkage culminating in a public notoriety as the examplar of the Durham County Council 'D' class villages (Warren 1973).

The introduction of the basic process to some extent, and even more the development of an efficient import trade for non-phosphoric ore, was followed by a noticeable slackening in the rate of growth of the output of steel on the North West coast which contained Britain's only important hematite ore bodies. At its peak the North West came within only a short distance of rivalling the North East coast, but by 1918 its output was less than one-fifth as much. Later, modifications to steelmaking techniques were associated with the entry of ironmaking districts of the Jurassic belt south of the Humber into steel. Steelmaking began in Scunthorpe in 1890 and was helped by the introduction of the tilting open hearth furnace which made it practicable to deal with the very high slag volumes associated with a low iron content and limy ore, and forty-five years later the Corby project was accompanied by important innovations in basic Bessemer practice.

The role of technical change in heavy chemicals was even clearer. The Leblanc process with its high raw material index and above all its large coal consumption built up the great focuses of Tyneside, Merseyside, and Clydeside. From at least the time of the Hemmings and Dyers patent of 1838 it was known that a technically simpler way of making alkali was possible by the saturation of a brine solution with ammonia. In the next decades this process was tried by Lancashire firms but they always gave up as commercial success seemed beyond them, mainly due to the high rate of loss of ammonia. Solvay's variant of the ammonia-soda process at Couillet in 1862 was followed by the establishment of works by Brunner and Mond in 1873 and commercial success in them by 1875—6. Use of brine rather than salt implied attraction to the saltfields, and economy in fuel consumption permitted this. The piping of brine for considerable distances was perfectly feasible—it had indeed been considered as much as fifty years earlier—but a combination of commitment in existing plant and processes and a relative lack of flexibility and initiative ensured that Widnes-St. Helens failed to adopt the new processes, and Northwich, where it was first successful, came to dominate the trade. In the North East the Tyneside alkali trade declined to extinction while the Teesside saltfield, known from 1862 but not worked for another twenty-two years, failed to develop anything more than a very small ammonia-soda operation which was ended before 1900 as a result of an agreement with Brunner and Mond. New technologies suggest new locations but the situation is permissive; it is variations in entrepreneurship which decided if and where these opportunities are taken up. This may be seen clearly in connection with shipbuilding.

Nineteenth-century shipbuilding with special reference to Thamesside and South Wales

As iron, and later steel, superseded wood, as steamships ousted sail, and as the whole complex of supply trades became more and more elaborate, there occurred a major concentration and locational shift in British shipbuilding. Although there seemed at first to be an inevitability associated with technical change about this process the changes were in fact complex (Jones 1957; Parkinson 1960).

'London, Sunderland, Newcastle, Hull, Liverpool, Yarmouth etc. are the great shipbuilding ports' wrote the economist McCulloch (1839), and the best ships were not then built on the northern or Scottish rivers. 'Ships built on the Thames enjoy the highest character; and generally, those built in the southern and western ports are said to be superior to those built on the Tyne and Wear . . . .' At that time there were a considerable number of shipbuilding centres around the coasts. Whitby and Bristol were major centres, building was still extensively carried on in the creeks and harbours of Hampshire, and within East Anglia not only were Harwich, Lowestoft, Ipswich, and King's Lynn active but so too were smaller centres like Wells on Sea (Lewis 1848). Yet even in this age of wooden building, local markets, massed capacity, and organizational excellence and enterprise—for instance in the purchase of wood—were pushing the northern rivers ahead rapidly. The Wear was especially prominent, its production rising from 7560 tons burden in 1820 to

51 823 by 1851. Steam vessels and a preference for iron boosted the
Tyne and particularly the Clyde. In the seven years up to 1852 247
steam vessels of a total burden of 147 604 tons were built on the Clyde:
only 14 (of 18 331 tons burden) had wooden hulls. In the early 1880s,
and with great rapidity, steel replaced iron—20 000 tons of steel shipping
was built in 1879, over 260 000 tons in 1883—and vessels grew in size and
complexity. Though many small, unmechanized yards survived both in
the great shipbuilding areas and elsewhere, access to ancillary engineering trades, to large supplies of cheap labour, and to shipbuilding steel
became important factors in yard survival (Cassell and Co. 1882). That
these were not in themselves sufficient factors is shown by the situation
of South Wales. Thamesside, by contrast, illustrates the struggle of a
district faced by a series of adverse developments.

   South Wales failed to become a major shipbuilder in the nineteenth
century, and, as a consequence, as a problem industrial area from the
1920s onwards had an even narrower industrial base than its two other
peripheral region rivals, central Scotland and North East England. In the
first half of the nineteenth century there was some shipbuilding. The
Neath Abbey Engine and Iron Shipbuilding Works was building ships in
the early fifties. There was no mention of shipbuilding at Cardiff then
but Swansea had both building and repair yards, and at Newport the
river was so situated '. . . that vessels of great burthen can be launched
from the docks into deep water' (*National Cyclopaedia* 1847–51).
Twenty years later Cardiff still had no significant yards, Swansea was
building and repairing, but in Newport shipbuilding was carried on 'to
a great extent' with six or seven yards. There were sail lofts, large anchor
and chain works, and so on there as well (*Imperial Gazeteer of England
and Wales* 1872; *Imperial Gazeteer* 1874). In the eighties and nineties
there seems to have been shrinkage of business in Newport though
several firms had taken up iron shipbuilding. Swansea building declined
and in the nineties its yards were confined to repairing. Cardiff by now
had not only dry docks but also large building and repair yards. By
1910 shipbuilding was merely one among many industries at Swansea
and Newport and was no longer in the lists of Cardiff industries
(*Encyclopaedia Britannica* 1875–87, 1911; *Comprehensive Gazeteer
of England and Wales* 1895). The failure of South Wales to develop in
shipbuilding is not easily explained (Table 3).

   There was a major growing coal export trade to stimulate local demand, and, even though in the heyday of the iron trade rails and bars
were dominant, some firms such as Dowlais even then produced iron
plate. The Cardiff works, built in 1890, was specially designed for steel

TABLE 3

Shipbuilding districts of England and Wales: 1889, 1906 (Production in thousands tons)

	1889	1906
Tyne, Blyth, and Whitby	306	394
Wear	217	335
Tees and Hartlepool	194	292
Mersey to Solway	77	24
Humber	22	38
Bristol Channel	10	2
Thames and miscellaneous		20

Sources: Engineering, 24 January 1890; *Shipbuilder,* winter 1907.

ship plate and deliberate attempts had already been made to start ship-building on a large scale there (I.C.T.R. 1882). Yet even though Cardiff works became an important factor in the supply of shipbuilding material to Irish Sea yards it never had a major local outlet. Explanations have never been fully satisfactory. Aberconway (1927) noted that South Wales lacked the necessary back-up engineering trades and, rather unconvincingly, suggested that the high wages paid in the ship repair docks of the coal ports would drive shipbuilding away. Almost certainly there was an important behavioural factor as well, the opposition to the Marquis of Bute to shipbuilding development there, though the reasons for his opposition again seem not to have been fully spelt out.

The Thames made the transition from high-class wooden to iron ship-building. By the early 1860s the Thames Iron Works and Shipbuilding Company consumed annually 8 to 10 000 tons of iron in its yards at the mouth of the Lea, making its own plates with as much as 10 000 tons of scrap collected in London and with the addition of some iron bar brought from the Milton Ironworks in the West Riding. (*Mechanics Magazine* 1861; Committee on Iron 1861–2). In the next twenty years there was a decline and by the early 1880s once famous yeards such as that at Millwall which had employed thousands were deserted. The names of London's marine engine firms—Maudsley, Humphreys, Penn and Russell—were still known throughout the world, but the shipyards were fewer; some like Samudas of Poplar and the Thames Ironworks concentrated largely on naval work, others, such as Greens, building for their own shipping line (Cassell & Co. 1882). Within a little over twenty years Samudas had closed, Thorneycrofts, formed at Chiswick in 1873, had moved to Southampton, and Yarrows, which had left the Isle of Dogs in 1901 for a new works at Poplar, five years later moved the whole establishment to Scotstoun on the Clyde. At the beginning of

1911 the Thames Ironworks, Shipbuilding, and Engineering Company
still employed 3000 and was not only building at Canning Town but had
laid out a new yard at Dagenham for fitting out and for building future
dreadnoughts. At the end of 1912 its works were closed by court order
and passed into receivership. Survival of the trade in the form of this
company for so long seems to have owed a great deal to the character
of the chairman, Arnold Hills (*The Times passim*; Aberconway 1927,
327). Remoteness from coal and steel was commonly argued as a major
cause of the decline of London's yards, though this was effectively
denied by the steel merchant Skelton (Skelton 1912). Deficiency in the
range of ancillary trades may have been a problem but the decisive
factor seems to have been in labour conditions—wages were too high
and labour relations were bad. The trend to shorter hours, and, with
Yarrow's move, problems over night-shift working were other factors
(*Royal Commission on the Depression of Trade and Industry* 1886).
Elsewhere in Britain shipyards sometimes survived, as at Appledore, or
collapsed, as at Whitby (Conzen 1958), for various almost fortuitious
reasons.

 Since the 1920s the growth of London and south eastern industrial
activity has been seen as a threat to the prosperity of the rest of Britain,
and indeed in the late 1930s the attitudes adopted to London frequently
cast it in a vampire-like role (Barlow Report 1940; Royal Geographical
Society 1938). It is well to recall that at the end of the nineteenth and
in the early years of the twentieth centuries there was a large-scale
migration of firms, particularly engineering firms, away from London
where land was expensive and labour costly. The importance of access
to coal and steel seems doubtful especially at a time when fuel use was
becoming more efficient and electricity was beginning to be employed.
Ferranti moved to Manchester, but other firms moving at this time
showed a marked preference for the East Midlands and outer parts of
the home counties. Brush Electric transferred from Lambeth to
Loughborough, Williams and Robinson of Thames Ditton in similar
trades moved to Rugby to works which later were operated by English
Electric. Ransome and Co. of Chelsea in 1901 and Simpson and Co. in
1924 moved to Newark, and while Peter Brotherhood moved from
Lambeth to Peterborough, Bryan Donkin of Bermondsey moved to
Chesterfield. A very significant move followed the absorption of
Alexander Wilson and Co. of Wandsworth by the Vauxhall Ironworks,
the removal to Luton in 1905 which laid the foundation for the Vauxhall automobile business there (Aberconway 1927, 323–8).

Integration of operations and location

Where trades were vertically integrated some manufacturing operations were located in places which were, or were believed generally to be, unsuitable. A notable modern example is the decision of Stewarts and Lloyds to build a large new blast furnace at their Bilston, Staffordshire, works in the early 1950s, a furnace which has for many years been the only surviving one in the Black Country. There are no district supplies of ore or coking coal but the benefits of hot metal practice to a steelmaking operation which played a vital role in the company's tube business were sufficient to justify the extra assembly costs—in effect, therefore, integration economies justified transfer cost disadvantages. In this once famous ironmaking district the Bilston project had a faintly anachronistic air. Quite different was the Ford Motor Company decision to build a blast furnace at Dagenham. This too was an example of backward integration, but it showed that a Thameside furnace could produce some of the lowest-cost iron in Britain. So fixed was the location pattern of the iron and steel industry, and perhaps so limited the perception of the industrial leaders, that in spite of the evidence of Dagenham's cost sheets no integrated operation has been built on Thameside in the succeeding forty-five years, though Stewards and Lloyds did consider a location there before opting for Corby, and Richard Thomas and Baldwins considered it for a possible strip mill before deciding on Newport in the late fifties.

Integration may be a beneficial factor in a works competitive situation or it may involve over extension and so reduce efficiency. Consett and Jarrow highlight the contrast. Consett Iron was integrated from coal and ore mines to finished steel, but did not go into steel-using trades. Palmers of Jarrow integrated backwards from ships to iron mines and collieries. From the discovery of the Cleveland orefield onwards Jarrow's location was better than Consett's. It had not only nearby coking coal collieries but direct unloading of ore—brought at nominal freight in returning colliers—and direct delivery of steel to the shipyards on the same site. Consett considered moving to the Tyne but instead chose to pioneer and to emphasize efficiency. Palmers meantime overextended and consequently could keep neither shipyard nor more particularly the iron and steel works in first-rate condition: they failed completely at the end of the twenties. Thirty years later Consett Iron opened a new ore dock on Jarrow Slake almost within sight of the old Palmers site. From here the ore was railed over twenty miles inland to Consett works more than 900 feet above sea level: much of its steel was sent down for further rolling at a mill built on part of the old Palmer's works. As far as commercial success is concerned locations are clearly permissive and not determinative. Some are ruled out as being by no strech of imagination within the margin of possible profitable operations: others, whether the current ideal, or less good now than in the past due to changes in material supply, markets, or techniques can be made resounding successes or costly failures depending upon the efficiency of management and men.

Regional growth, stagnation, and diversification

Trade specialisms emerge as firms serve a common market or use common materials. Reputation and trade associations may reinforce this localization. Once they are established, activities tend to be perpetuated. However, they also evolve in various ways, grow relatively faster or slower than others, diversify or remain narrowly based, and the district economy expands faster or slower. This applies at both the national and the regional levels, former prominence in activity may decline, old leaders are displaced. The principle of secular stagnation which Rostow expounded is of great geographical value.

The popular view until World War I saw Britain as the continuing workshop for the world. 'The British Isles owe their political and industrial supremacy to natural conditions', the Harmsworth Press assured its Edwardian readers, 'The mildness of their climate, their favourable position, nearly in the centre of the Land Hemisphere, their numerous admirable harbours, and their immense natural resources, especially in coal and iron, caused them almost of necessity to become the most important manufacturing country of the world' (Harmsworth *c.* 1907). A quarter of a century before, another popularizer had been even more convinced of British primacy, but had with considerable insight seen also some of the wider geographical implications

Great Britain and her brilliant dependencies form an industrial empire pure and simple. It is their business and function in the world to be industrial just as it is the business of other empires to be agricultural and warlike. Year after year, what the Americans would call our 'manifest destiny' is driving us faster and faster into this position—forcing us to withdraw from merely producing raw material, and to concentrate more and more our energies on the business of furnishing the world with that raw material transformed into finished goods. England (sic) is year by year becoming the artisan, the spinner, the weaver, the shipbuilder, the manufacturer, the engineer of the world. The world is every year more and more becoming a sort of colossal agriculturalist, to render marketable whose productions is the business of the factories and factory hands of England. (Cassell and Co. 1882, i, 1).

Nationally, the structure, though so magnificent, was rotting, there was too much lumber from the past.

In chemicals it was Germany's progress above all which earliest exposed the deficiencies of British practice: in steel too the Germans were prominent but the pace here was made by the Americans. Customs duties and other external circumstances were less important factors in decline than the more careful scientific training of managers and chemists (Lunge 1893; Chemical Trade Journal 1888). A few years later the English chemist Thorpe (1895) had to admit 'One of the greatest object lessons in so-called technical education that I know if is to be seen on the banks of the Rhine at Ludwigshafen . . .' in steel the story is much more fully documented (Burn 1940 *passim*; Billy and Melius 1904). Here too there were a multitude of factors, and commentators too often went for simplistic explanations such as that of Kirchhoff (1900) who suggested that selective emigration over a century had taken away the best talent and energy, particularly from the workers.

The stagnation which was seen at the national level also frequently characterized regions: an old leader which had long ago overcome the special difficulties or had reaped the full benefits from its particular mineral endowment typically passed on, as its pioneers aged, into slower growth and less adaptability. So in turn, in iron, South Wales was superseded by Scotland which by the 1870s had lost its growth impetus as Cleveland became dominant. However, another principle comes in at this point, namely the diversification of a regional economy which may take it to a new, higher level of economic maturity, a few basic trades leading through eventually to a complex manufacturing economy. Of the coal and iron districts a few failed almost completely to follow this course. Lincolnshire and Northamptonshire, coming late into the field when finishing trades were already well developed elsewhere, were notable instances. Although iron and steel, as a mayor of Scunthorpe remarked not many years ago, has built up an industrial district of some 120 000, it has made Scunthorpe itself, as the heart of this district, into a one-horse town. The steel industry on the rather isolated north west coast followed a similar course. On a much bigger scale South Wales remained to a dangerous degree merely a coal-steel-tinplate area. At the beginning of Welsh industrialization David Williams (1796) had looked at a process of snowball growth. 'By the construction of furnaces and collieries, the formation of railroads and canals, a hilly district of great extent will soon be productive of incalculable wealth, and on the banks of the canal [the Monmouthshire Canal] from Pontypool to Newport a second Birmingham will arise as if by enchantment.' This growth cycle was atrophied. In central Scotland the process was carried much further, further indeed than on the North East coast. There an interesting sub-regional contrast had emerged by the 1860s, a contrast which is still prominent today, between the iron- and steelmaking district of Cleveland and the more complex economy of Tyneside. In 1863 a survey of engineering—excluding shipbuilding, but not marine engineering—in the north east showed that of 14 leading firms, 10 were on the Tyne, 1 on the Wear, and 3 at Hartlepool or on the Tees. Employment in the three districts was respectively 7624, 200 1650 (Westmacott and Spencer 1863). As late as 1880 almost two-thirds of the pig iron of the Cleveland district was sent out of the district un-manufactured (*Colliery Guardian* 1880).

In the West Midlands the process of economic growth and diversifi-cation, the building of one trade on another, replacement of dying by new activities, reached its peak. Aberconway attributed this to the early pre-eminence of the area (Aberconway 1927, 291) but there were other factors. One was its early and major regional markets, another the high quality of its iron. Furthermore, competitive pressures forced it into new lines while other major coal and iron rivals still had ample resources to draw on in the older, unsophisticated lines. The result was a bewilderingly complex metalworking economy which contained the growth prospects for twentieth-century West Midland economic dynamism. Aberconway (1927, 291) merely hinted at the complexity of south Staffordshire trades:

. . . materials for bridge and constructional engineering, railway carriage and wagon building, heavy foundry and iron and steel works machinery, chilled and grain rolls, electrical engineering, nuts and bolts, tubes . . . locks, wood screws, ship's chain, cable and anchors, cast iron holloware, and stamped tinned and enamelled holloware.

When a complex structure did not exist, it could to some extent be created. The attempts, notably by James Ramsden, to widen the economic base of Barrow in Furness are an excellent example (Marshall 1958; Ramsden 1897). Even before the terrible troubles of the north east coast iron trade in the 1870s the local press was convinced that '. . . it was of paramount importance to get new industries to be located on the banks of the Tees'. Discovery of the saltfields in 1862 seemed to promise diversification—'we have no reason to be dissatisfied with what ironstone has done for us, and we anticipate scarecely less important results to flow from the development of salt' (*North Eastern Gazette* 1869). Sometimes the diversification had to be forced if it was to come at all. In two chemical towns, Widnes in 1897 and Northwich two years later, public meetings were held to consider the ways in which their economies might be diversified. Clothing and boot and shoe manufacture were suggested for the first, in the case of the second discussion ranged over soap, cotton, pottery, jam, argicultural implements, milk, bacon factories, and so on (*Chemical Trade Journal* 1897, 1899). In discussing the Widnes situation the Chemical Trade Journal interestingly recognized '. . . it is difficult to force the growth of a town in an old country like this, where trade has settled into certain grooves and localities'.

Economic growth and environment

The Victorians had a love-hate relationship with industrialization and with the landscapes it created, though gradually a distaste for the more extreme effects came to dominate. They wrote with no obvious feeling of incongruity of the transformation of pastoral scenes into built-up, industrialized urban complexes, of Elswick works built out into the Tyne beyond the point where Lord Armstrong used to fish under the willows when he was a boy (*Engineer* 1889), of Saville Street, Sheffield, as a former 'Sylvan retreat' where Sir John Brown could '. . . recall with pleasure the blue bells which used to flourish in the woods opposite to his counting-house windows'(!) (Dunbar 1882). Sometimes it seemed almost that the industrialization of landscapes was a good thing. The *Athenaum* speculated in 1879 how beautiful the wooded valleys and unfouled waters of the five rivers which met in Sheffield must have been, but now '. . . it would perhaps be hard to find a more prosaic or a more unpleasant place'. From above the Sheaf one now looked down upon '. . . a dense and seething mass of human activity with its modern accompaniment of smoke and flame, and ceaseless roar' (Hibbs 1882). The American Abram Hewitt had no doubt at all as he travelled near Wolverhampton in 1844: 'This is the most wonderful country you can possibly conceive of. It is like one continuous town, so populous it is. Thousands and thousands of furnaces are everywhere casting forth their black and blackening smoke . . .' (Nevins 1935). Some, it is true, saw that all was not well when industry abused all the landscape in this way. As early as the 1820s Baron Charles Dupin alluded to the anomalous situation in the Black Country '. . . where the most striking picture of destruction, results from an industry of which the productive force shows what fortunate power the genius of modern people exercises over nature' (Dupin 1826). In 1859 Ruskin (1907) saw things even clearer, and by inference rejected the 'workshop of the world' philosophy referred to above. 'All England may, if it so chooses, become one manufacturing town: and Englishmen, sacrificing themselves to the good of general humanity, may live diminished lives in the midst of noise, of darkness, and of deadly exhalation.'

The heavy industry of the nineteenth century gave Britain the power to develop the greatest of empires. The momentum from that industrialization is one of the most important factors enabling it to maintain one of the world's highest income levels three-quarters of a century later when many of both its natural and acquired advantages have gone. In the process industrialization changed the economic geography of Britain, the location of industry, the flows of materials and finished products, the distribution of population, the relationship between town and country. It transformed the landscape and handed on a host of problems as well as assets to the twentieth century—fixed points in the industrial map, and too many of them as well, old company structures and old communities, both with notions which it was difficult to adjust to the very different needs of a new world order. All these are regarded here as aspects of the geography of heavy industry. There remains one more, the active principle, the movement from study to action, the role of applied geography in transforming the legacy of a materialist past into something more in accordance with ideals for the future. Though his own progeny was to prove a catastrophic falling-away from the ideal, and the very grounds of his philosophy are repugnant to many of us, this task was nowhere better summed up than by another eminent mid-Victorian, Karl Marx (1845), 'Philosophers have only interpreted the world in various ways, but the real task is to alter it.'

4 Evolution and intervention in heavy industry location patterns

Product evolution and comparative advantage

The genesis of Morris Motors was in the little shop in Oxford where William Morris began to repair bicycles in 1893. This is one example of a process of wide importance in location, especially in an old industrial country—evolution from one product to another with the location, though not necessarily the site, remaining unchanged. Product evolution is a particular case of the general principle of comparative advantages. Such advantages have to be perceived before changes occur; industrial patterns evolve as well as take shape in the first instance because of behavioural factors.

The factors which affected the location decisions for the original trade may not be ideal for the new one, but on the basis of established work forces and skills, goodwill and local trading connections, and perhaps some plant from the first trade which may be usable in the second, the new activity is begun and successfully carried on in a less than theoretically optimum location. The extremely complex metal-working economy of the West Midlands exemplifies this at both the individual plant and regional level. The still major steel tube trade of the region is allegedly the modern derivative of the famous Wednesbury gun barrel business which had surplus capacity after the Napoleonic Wars at a time when demand for water and gas pipes for expanding urban areas was mounting rapidly. In turn the tube business provided a market for a new finished iron line, that of iron strip, and so the effects ramified through to ironmaking and mineral working (Allen 1929, *passim*). At the end of the Victorian age product evolution in the same region was laying its foundations for twentieth-century metalworking and engineering trades among the relics of older primary activities. In 1871 there were 61 pig-iron-making plants in the Black Country with 165 blast furnaces. By 1890 only 31 works with 85 blast furnances survived, of which well under one-third were at work (*J.I.S.I.* 1871; *Mineral Statistics of the United Kingdom* 1890). Between 1890 and 1906 the number of finished (malleable) iron works in the Black Country fell from 121 to 83 (Rylands 1890 and 1906). Given the already diverse metalworking structure of the region, its high-class iron production and perhaps its central location, this decline fostered new growth industries. Cycles were one—with new demands for tubes—but either independently or from cycle trades there was movement on to motor cycles and cars and to component manufacture. Fisher and Ludlow had begun making tinmen's furniture and holloware fittings in Birmingham in 1851. In 1913 they entered the automobile trade with first motor cycle and then automobile pressings. Until after World War II they operated over a dozen works in and around Birmingham but in 1947 they concentrated operations on a new plant at Castle Bromwich (S.M.I. 1947). With a major shift of site but not of location a tinmen's furniture manufacturer in 1851 had become by 1975 one of B.L.M.C.'s chronic problems of operation.

Over an equal length of time industrial evolution and new interregional connections in semi-finished material movement transformed Sheffield. In the second quarter of the nineteenth century the growth of the railway systems not only changed space relationships between heavy industrial districts but also provided new opportunities for iron manufacturers. The market for best Yorkshire iron expanded as Leeds and Bradford firms built their boiler plate mills and the bulk demand for rails made Welsh and later Cleveland fortunes. On an initially more modest scale Sheffield firms were turning out quality steels for the railway age. Among these firms three, John Browns, Cammells, and Vickers, grew and evolved outstandingly. In the 1860s Cammells and a little later John Browns pioneered in bulk steelmaking in the form of Bessemer rail production, but within twenty years intrinsically beter endowed districts, notably South Wales, Teesside, Barrow, and west Cumberland had pushed their way into the business. In response the Sheffield firms turned to the production of armour plate and armaments, to big castings and forgings, and particularly to marine work, the specialization which eventually through merger and purchase brought them all into major shipbuilding—Browns at Clydebank, Cammells at Birkenhead, and Vickers at Barrow. In this case special steels, closely allied to the traditional cutlery trades, had been supplanted by a twenty-year period of mass-production low-grade steels and then by a reversion to special steels, not now, in the case of these major firms, small goods but massive, heavy products. In 1894–5, for instance, these three firms together received government orders for 23 000 tons of armour plate (Stainton 1924). Even so these were high-value products and in that respect they reaffirmed Sheffield's quality emphasis. By the mid-1920s Aberconway estimated that in busy times the value of the steel produced in Sheffield was probably equal to that of the rest of England (Aberconway 1927, 58, 59). But as the product lines evolved and the space relationships of Sheffield firms with other parts of industrial Britain became more complicated, so too Attercliffe and Brightside, whose valley flats had grown crops of wheat in the early days of Cammell's Cyclops Works, grew rapidly. The township of Brightside and Attercliffe had 2944 inhabited houses in 1841; 50 years later they had increased to 20 751. In this process of growth they became the dense mass of congested, intermingled works, drab, flat, long streets and dusty, undistinguished housing which has come down as a major physical planning problem to the late twentieth century.

Product evolution has also been pronounced in shipbuilding. The Tyne and Wear first made their mark in wooden collier building but not only did they later move on to iron and steel and from sail to steam but there too, in the archetypal homeland of coal, there began the evolution of the modern oil tanker. Oil-carrying vessels were built on the Tyne as early as 1863, and in 1886 Armstrongs built the first of the recognizably modern-style tankers, the *Gluckhauf* (*Encyclopaedia Britannica* 1911; McCord and Rowe 1971). Appropriately enough, in 1969 the Tyne launched the first British supertanker of one-quarter million tons. On the Clyde product evolution at the old John Browns yard had by the early 1970s taken it wholly out of shipbuilding into oil rig construction.

In Eastern England there occurred a very different but important process of industrial evolution. There, at the end of the eighteenth century or in the first half of the nineteenth century, agricultural machinery productionwas begun in a considerable number of market towns to meet regional needs. Increases in the cost of farm labour, as manufacturing provided competitive job outlets, helped more and more to extend the demand for machinery. A multitude of local or regional shows, and from 1839 the show of the Royal Agricultural Society, held annually in different parts of the country, publicized their progress.

Some of the machinery was produced in the coal, iron, and engineering districts—Leeds, for instance, was an important centre—some came from market towns in the south and west, such as Banbury or Exeter, but the biggest agglomeration of capacity was in the eastern agricultural districts. Works here obtained their coal and iron by rail or by water from the older, bigger engineering districts to the west and north. Some of the new agricultural machinery centres were important railway junctions, such as Bedford. Others, though on the edge of great grain districts, were well located for rail delivery of raw materials as at Gainsborough, Lincoln, Newark, and Grantham. Leiston and Ipswich, though remote by rail, were able to bring in their coal and iron along the coast. In many instances agricultural machinery production revived a stagnant economy, pushed it to new high levels and, as product evolution occurred, left the eastern towns as general engineering centres.

Gainsborough's population fell by 13 per cent to 6320 between 1851 and 1861 largely because of a movement away of watermen and rope makers, but by the mid-nineties Marshall's Britannia Works there alone employed about 3000 in manufacturing agricultural machinery, steam boilers, and engines. Population at the 1891 census was 14 000. By that time Ipswich had four notable engineering works among which Ransome's Orwell Works ranked as one of the largest agricultural machinery firms in Britain. Garrett's works in Leiston was founded as early as 1788 but grew rapidly only in the mid-nineteenth century. By the early 1870s, when the works employed 600, the population of the town was only 2227, though this was an increase of almost 50 per cent since 1850. Lincoln in 1851 had 17 000 inhabitants but forty years later had 41 000 when its engineering and agricultural implement firms were said to be 'world famous'—one alone had made over 23 000 engines and as many threshing machines (*Imperial Gazeteer* 1872; *Comprehensive Gazeteer of England and Wales* 1895). Before the end of the century Lincoln firms had begun to set up overseas branches and to diversify into general engineering. They became renowned for excavators, marine boilers, pumps, and so on. Shortly after World War I engineering trades there employed 8000 men. Aberconway (1927, 79) summarized the structure of this district when he observed that east of the London to York main line 20 000 were in engineering employment, and the capital engaged was almost as much as that in shipbuilding and engineering on the North East coast.

Whereas product evolution brought new trades to old areas it usually involved the same broad category of activity—steelmaking or engineering and so on. The wider, more general principle of comparative advantage sometimes caused a new activity to replace a wholly dissimilar line. It worked when entrepreneurs, companies, or investors realized that transfer of capital from an old specialism to a new one gave sufficiently higher returns to justify the inconvenience. Regional impact occurred when this was so generally obvious that many groups acted at the same time in the same direction. New raw material discoveries or technical change were frequently the instruments of such a decisive swing of advantage. The relationship between the textile and the metal industries provides an interesting case, one which was of very considerable importance in the nineteenth century. A local instance and a regional example will be considered.

Before the opening of the Stockton and Darlington Railway in 1825 made it a link in the chain of movement from the coal-pits around Witton Park to the Tees and Stockton, Darlington was a small market town best known for its flax, linen, and worsted trades. As branches were built from Stockton and Darlington, both eastwards and within the coalfield, its importance increased, and the building of the York and Newcastle Railway gave it a new role as a major rail junction before the end of the 1840s. The Pease family in particular invested wealth made in Darlington textile mills in railway extension and in the development of Middlesbrough as a coal port, also widely in coal mines, and after 1850 in opening mines and railways in Cleveland. Within the south west Durham/Cleveland coal/iron ore pattern of movement Darlington began to build up major railway equipment, engineering, and finished iron trades. The market for iron which they constituted brought blast furnaces to the town. Linen manufacture which had employed 500 looms declined, though as late as the mid-1870s the Pease family still owned 270 looms there, employing 700 people. By the end of the century there was no mention of looms, but worsted spining in Pease mills still provided 500 to 600 jobs. By 1870 iron works and wagon works, and later bridge building and locomotive building—rationalizing, the North Eastern had centralized all its loco work there by the early twentieth century—became dominant activities. Moreover, in addition to transforming its own industrial structure, capital originally made in Darlington textiles played a key role in the mineral and metallurgical devolopment of South Durham and Teesside—the Pease interests along employed (6500 in producing 3 million tons of minerals annually by the mid-seventies (McCulloch 1866; *Encyclopaedia Britannica* 1877 and 1902).

The working-out of comparative advantage in Lancashire and Lanarkshire textiles is more contentious. There were certainly endowment factors in the process. Even if, nowadays, the positive advantages of soft waters derived from the millstone grit or natural humidity which checks the breaking of cotton thread are discounted, Lancashire had negative factors in its relatively poor endowment in Coal Measure iron ore and coking coal (Hull 1862; Meade 1882). Iron, steel, and engineering trades grew out of Lancashire's primary preoccupation with textiles. They were not a 'natural' development from mineral resources as in the Black Country. At a later date industrial divergence took some of these industries far from their original activities. Warrington wire works, perhaps initially a response to the needs for wool-combing, continued to expand when that had become an insignificant part of their market. A textile machinery firm such as Mather and Platt of Oldham was in numerous other engineering lines by the end of the century, and the links with other north western industries were becoming more complex—in the mid-1890s, for instance, the firm built much of the new Castner-Kellner electrolytic alkali works at Runcorn, and William Mather, Mather and Platt's chairman became chairman of that company's board. The manufacturing range of Manchester or of many of the cotton towns—for instance, Bolton as described by Aberconway in the 1920s—is indicative of the complex structure which may evolve even in a region of initially specialized activity (Iron and Steel Institute 1935).

In central Scotland, and especially in Lanarkshire, a large cotton textile industry was swamped in the nineteenth century by the rising coal, iron, and engineering trades. Here there were a damp atmosphere, a traditional textile labour force, good trading connections through the Clyde, and a number of ancillary trades such as the great Tennant bleach works at St. Rollox. Even so the endowment for the mineral and metal trades was even better. Raw coal (splint) suitable for smelting, blackband iron ore made usable by the introduction of the hot blast, the whole knit together by the Monkland and Forth and Clyde canals and later by a railway network, along with a tremendous success in interregional and still more international trade in iron, and the growth of mechanical engineering and shipbuilding to give a home market—all these constituted an incentive to transfer factors of production from textiles to metals. After a peak in mid-century the cotton textile industry stagnated and then drifted downwards. In 1838 Scotland had 35·6 thousand cotton operatives as compared with 188·6 thousand in Lancashire and Cheshire; by 1898–9 the respective numbers were 29·0 and 432·4 thousand. In one or two instances it is possible to see the process of comparative advantage working out in Scotland. Henry Houldsworth learned spinning in Manchester after 1792. In the late nineties he sold yarn in Glasgow and in 1801 became a proprietor of a cotton mill there. A little later he put up another mill at Anderston on the west side of Glasgow. Anderston was equipped with a machine shop for its own needs and later turned out work for other mill owners. Eventually Houldsworth abandoned spinning and as the foundry and machine business expanded bought into the iron ore and coal trade. In 1837 he formed the Coltness Iron Company which played an important role in the Scotch iron industry both in Lanark and Ayrshire and was an important colliery concern until nationalization of British mining (Carvell 1948).

In the 1830s Houldsworth had built his third textile mill in Airdrie and here in mid-century the gradual transfer from textiles to coal, iron, and engineering may be traced (Macarthur 1890). To the end of the century it retained traces of textile-making but had become mainly preoccupied with metal industries. By the mid-twentieth century these old staples had in turn decayed, and, behind windows artistically etched

with the names of mid-Victorian engineers, new concerns were making
new consumer products—an old wire rope factory producing potato
crisps and another works producing ice cream wafers (Hogg 1958).

Elsewhere the pressures of a definitely contracting trade rather than
the opportunities of another forced transfer of activities. This seems to
have been the case in Wales, where, as steel with its bigger scales of
production and need for low phosphorous ore replaced puddled iron,
the North Crop works were increasingly disadvantaged. Some just failed,
others went over to coal sales, and by the early years of the twentieth
century the tips and sidings of some of the most successful Welsh colliery
companies occupied the sites of former furnaces and forges. The financial
incentive to such a change may be appreciated by the experience of
Tredegar. Over a long period it had averaged a dividend of only 3¼ per
cent; in the five years after the iron and steel works was scrapped the
dividend was 6½ per cent (Aberconway 1927, 248–50, 269). Interestingly, however, there was also in this instance a long-term legacy to
South Wales metallurgy. The old Tredegar mill was converted to become
a pioneer British Morgan continuous mill and this was so successful as a
rerolling operation that it financed the new Whitehead mills of Newport
in the early 1920s and a decade later the transfer of the Tredegar operations to Scunthorpe. Both plants still exist.

Some locations were the result of entrepreneurship held in common
rather than of comparative advantage or process evolution, and sometimes this meant that giant iron and engineering concerns went on into
activities for which their locations were not at all favourable. This may
be seen in the industrial activities of Bell Brothers of North East England,
a firm dominated for fifty years by Isaac Lowthian Bell, an internationally renowned metallurgical authority. From association with iron and
chemicals at Walker on Tyne and at Washington on the Wear, Bells went
on in 1852 to start the Port Clarence Ironworks on Teesside. In the
1880s they began salt manufacture and went on a modest scale into the
ammonia-soda method of soda ash production—by a process which
proved much less efficient than Solvay's. At Washington between 1860
and 1874 they produced aluminium before the Hall-Héroult electrolytic
process swept away the rationale for coalfield locations, and moved the
industry to hydroelectric power sites in Scotland and then overseas. Not
only did Bells thus set up a series of eventually unsuccessful operations
but their overextensions were probably one factor in their failure to
keep pace with newcomers in Teesside iron and steel. The overextension
can be sensed by the tone of Bell Brothers Minute Books (Bell Brothers).

Immediately after World War I an interesting case of association of
unlike activities occurred as many engineering firms, trying to find

employment for plants which had been so greatly extended in wartime, forced their way into the automobile business. Most of these were in suboptimal or downright poor locations. Difficult trading conditions and the mass production pioneered at this time by bigger, more established, and better located producers, quickly weeded them out in the mid-twenties. Between 1916 and 1925, 125 firms entered the automobile manufacturing business, 35 of them outside the Midlands–South East focus of the industry. At this time South Wales (Cardiff) secured its only automobile plant before the government-inspired devolution of the sixties. Rustons of Lincoln and Armstrong-Whitworth on Tyneside were among those who began to produce private cars. Survival value was low and each of these locations left the industry between 1921 and 1925. In the years 1925 to 1930 the number of new entrants to the trade had fallen to 18 of which only 3 were outside the Midland-South East section of the Axial Belt (Littlewood 1962–3).

Rationalization and the geography of heavy industry

In the years around 1900 big, national industrial concerns, sometimes with many plants, became a dominating feature in British heavy industry. They emerged partly as a response to international challenges, partly as a result of difficulties in trade at home, and partly as a reflection of new opportunities to improve profitability. To some extent the latter was the result of the gradual supercession of classical perfect competition by imperfect competition sometimes leading to oligopoly, to some extent, however, it was the result of increased operational efficiency resulting from plant specialization and scale economies. Inevitably also some smaller, less efficient, or poorly located plants were closed and in some cases new ones were built.

The first giant British merger, one which indeed produced a firm which briefly claimed to be the biggest business unit in the world, was in the heavy chemical trades where, in 1890, almost the whole of the Leblanc alkali industry came together to form the United Alkali Company. Forty-six works were wholly acquired and the Leblanc departments of five others. Almost immediately U.A.C. closed some of its less successful plants and thereby noticeably speeded the decline of the once major alkali trade of Tyneside and increasing still further the relative importance of the Merseyside centres of the trade. Table 4 illustrates this process in the first decade for alkali works only and excluding the few salt and metal recovery works which were also included in the initial forty-six works (U.A.C.). U.A.C. built two important new works in the first decade, both of them using the ammonia-soda process to produce soda ash,

TABLE 4

United Alkali Company: distribution of works acquired in 1890 and closures 1890–5 and 1896–1900

	Widnes	St. Helens	Runcorn-Weston	Liverpool
Acquired 1890	14	8 (1)	4	1
Closed to 1895	2	3	–	–
Closed 1896–1900	2	2	–	1

	Flint	Bristol	Dublin	Scotland	North East
Acquired 1890	1 (1)	1	1 (2)	4	9 (1)
Closed to 1895	(1)	–	1 (2)	1	4
Closed 1896–1900	–	–	–	–	1

N.B. ( ) indicates works whose Leblanc department only was acquired.
Source: U.A.C. records.

Fleetwood, built on the newly opened saltfield in 1892, and a works at Bay City, Michigan, opened in 1896 in order to avoid the troublesome increased American tariffs. Gradually U.A.C. widened its product range until it had a bewilderingly complex list. Leblanc alkali production was completely extinct by the early twenties, but although the formation of I.C.I. in 1926 was followed by a further round of closures a number of old U.A.C. works still exist though with different products. The Widnes district is a particularly notable instance.

There were 124 separate railway companies in Britain in 1914. The creation of the four big railway groups in 1921 and of British Railways twenty-six years later was followed by a protracted and still not completed process of concentration of railway workshop activity. In shipbuilding, where private ownership continued, concentration was even slower. As late as 1941 the United Kingdom still had 60 large shipyards. The Clyde had 40 yards in the mid-1880s and in 1941 there were still 22 in which employment ranged from a few hundred to 7000 (Bellerby 1943). Since World War II the process of rationalization has gathered momentum. There were 40 shipbuilding firms on the North East Coast in the mid-1920s: fifty years later merger has cut those of any considerable size to 3. Rationalization of yards as opposed to firms has proved much more difficult, so that there still remain some 15 of these. Even in this case, however, specialization has been possible and individual yards can provide specific services for the operations of the whole group (Warren 1973).

In steel the formation of big groups was particularly important in the early years of the twentieth century, but although a few plants were then closed—for instance Cyfarthfa by G.K.N. and Tudhoe by the South

Durham group—any thoroughgoing rationalization was delayed for a quarter of a century. At that time the biggest regional groupings not only extended their control but increased plant specialization and abandoned a number of units such as Clarence on Teesside, Dowlais, Mossend, Calderbank, Wigan, and Penistone. Unfortunately from the point of view of the later international competitiveness of British Steel too many suboptimal locations were preserved and rebuilt. Sometimes individual companies were to blame, but frequently this was the outcome of the work of trade associations.

Trade associations frequently have limited production or fixed prices so as to benefit all producers. The result has been to keep marginal plants in production, at least for a time as with the Bleaching Powder Association or the Galvanised Iron Trade associations in the 1880s (Warren 1970). The price agreements in the middle of the next decade between the U.A.C. and its great rivals Brunner and Mond and Solvay et cie helped to perpetuate the life of U.A.C.'s less competitive units, and therefore enabled some of them located in accordance with the factors affecting the Leblanc trade to survive to become important in other lines of business. The International Rail Syndicate not only allocated quotas but sometimes paid firms to keep out of production. The decline and then the elimination of Darlington as a steel centre in the 1890s was eased from the point of view of the company, but clearly not from the point of view of the work force, by such a payment. Conversely, in the 1930s the British Iron and Steel Federation made arrangements which kept a greater number of plants at work than was desirable. Its aim was '. . . to meet the position of certain high-cost producers whose outputs are essential in busy periods, but whose costs are too high to be used to determine the price level'. (I.D.A.C. 1937).

A case of association and regulation of especial interest and locational importance concerns the section of the heavy steel trade producing ship plate and angles. In 1885–6 an agreement between four leading steel-makers produced the Scottish Steelmakers Association, a body which, except for short periods, remained important for many years, and through which the poorly located and inadequately integrated Scottish firms protected themselves against English competition. The Association virtually abolished local competition. In the early years of the century it came to an agreement with North of England makers of the same products whereby each was given undisputed access to markets in certain regions of the country. Midland plate-makers joined the agreement, but there remained some outsiders, notably Cardiff works. An important result was that whereas Clyde shipbuilders in particular had to pay the high association price for their steel, Cardiff sold at well below association prices, particularly in Irish Sea markets and most notably of all in Belfast. As a result Harland and Wolff and Workman Clarke, the two big yards there, were able to more than cancel out their apparent disadvantageous location away from iron and steelworks and become, as far as steel was concerned, low cost builders (Macrosty 1907; Levy 1927). Much later, in the 1950s and 1960s, the system of 'zonal extras' over base prices for its products adopted by the members of the British Iron Steel Federation completely reversed the situation with Harland and Wolff paying extra over the prices for plate and angles in the British heavy steel districts.

The creation of National Shipbuilders Security Ltd. in 1930 was an example of an association formed to force through rationalization. Its policy was to buy up yards, dismantle them, and to ensure when disposing of the site that it should not be used again for shipbuilding for at least forty years. By the end of 1934 it had scrapped 137 berths with about one million tons annual building capacity, an extraordinary Draconian policy which left only about 1·4 million tons capacity in important yards (Hallsworth 1935). Among the yards which were closed were Beardmore's at Dalmuir which was for a time considered as a possible estuarine steelworks site (*Glasgow Herald* 1938) and the Palmers yard at Jarrow well down river among the shipyards of the Tyne, the only one in Britain fully integrated backwards to ironmaking and the sole major prop of the economy of the town of Jarrow.

Government action and location

Long before socially motivated policies for regional development became important governments affected location decisions indirectly through fiscal and tariff policies. An important example of the first was the Salt Tax imposed by Pitt in 1798 as a source of revenue. The duty was increaed to 75p a bushel in 1805, reduced to 10p in 1823, and repealed in 1825. Its existence had delayed the emergence of a salt- and coal-based alkali industry using Leblanc's process, and had conversely helped to build up alkali manufacture based on kelp-burning in the western and northern isles. Repeal removed one of the important props of the crofting economy and set in train the growth of the chemical complexes of Clydeside, Tyneside, and Merseyside.

Tariff policy later became a locational factor of first importance. This was clearly the case in the world situation of Britain, affecting whether industrial expansion took place there or overseas. Protection permitted overseas competitors to extend their own heavy trades, first capitalizing on richer raw materials or cheaper labour and then becoming lower-cost producers by virtue of newer equipment than in Britain or eventually because of larger scales of operation. In the mid-1870s there was scarcely any effective foreign competition for British shipyards, but by the 1880s overseas protection was causing alarm. Passenger and mail steamers for German lines had been built in Britain but the German government had required that six large vessels being built for North German Lloyd in spring 1886 should be built at home and of German steel. In Stettin where they were being constructed, elsewhere in North Germany and also in Denmark, Sweden, Norway, and Holland material could be obtained quite as cheaply as on the Tyne, and wages—which over the past twenty years had increased steadily in proportion to total costs—were still much lower. Angle men in Kiel and Stettin were then getting 26¼p a day as compared with 60p in North East England (Price 1886, 145).

Germany, France, and the Russian Empire during the last twenty years of the nineteenth century and the United States in the nineties built up their new Solvay capacity behind substantial tariff barriers. Duties on imported agricultural machinery not only caused British firms to build overseas branches but thereby also restricted expansion of plant in the market towns of Eastern England. However, this did not necessarily check their further growth for it may have encouraged the process of diversification which carried some of them wholly out of agricultural into general engineering.

While others imposed import duties Britain struggled on with free trade and this too had locational impact, particularly in steel. At the end of the 1890s German and American firms, having become big and efficient behind their protective barriers, were able to begin to sell in Britain at lower prices than British firms could meet. In the first years of the twentieth century the trickle of imported steel became a flood. Not only did this help to bolster the British shipyards but the importance of semi-finished steel encouraged a reorientation of the rerolling branch of the steel industry to coastal districts. The completely new prominence of Newport, Monmouthshire, as an important metallurgical centre was achieved over the first twenty years of the new century as three major rerolling concerns moved in: Lysaghts from the West Midlands, Mannesmann with a branch of its Ruhr tube business, and Whiteheads with its bar business previously confined to Tredegar. Other interior firms moved to coastal locations in the North West, making Ellesmere Port, Widnes— where in one case an abandoned alkali works site was chosen—and Hawarden Bridge into important metalworking locations. In the last instance a location chosen for rerolling imported steel for export markets became within sixty years a fully integrated works pre-eminently concenred with home demand and was eventually handed on as a 2 million ton works to become one of the major problems in rationalization by the British Steel Corporation.

Abandonment of free trade affected locational values and choices just as much as its maintenance had done. Steel tariff protection in 1932 was followed by a commitment on the part of the industry to rationalize. An early result was the creation in 1934 of the British Iron and Steel Federation as a new co-ordinating body for the industry. Although B.I.S.F. did much valuable work one unfortunate result was the reinforcement of a 'live and let live' philosophy which helped to perpetuate and modernize too many old locations (Carr and Taplin 1962; Burn 1940, 1961; Vaizey 1974). Too many new mills were built on old sites, some excellent as on south Teesside, some of very doubtful long-term viability as at Clydebridge or Cardiff or, as with Ebbw Vale, undoubtedly very bad from the point of view of commercial considerations. The cutting-off of the easy importation of large supplies of basic Bessemer steel especially suitable for tube strip was the occasion for Stewarts and Lloyds to embark on the project which they had already planned for some years, the construction of Corby works.

Direct government intervention in location decisions came only in the twentieth century, but well before that government action had been instrumental in keeping some locations alive. The role of A. J. Mundella, M.P. for a Sheffield constituency from 1868 to 1897, and President of the Board of Trade in 1886, is interesting in this respect. In 1884 when there was a plan to build large new armament capacity at Woolwich, Mundella pointed out that Brightside firms were quite willing to supply national needs. On a number of occasions after this he ensured that the government fulfilled its commitment of 1884 to place gun forging orders with Vickers, Firths, and Cammells (Stainton 1924, 45). Naval orders kept Thamesside shipbuilding alive into the early years of the twentieth century. In the thirties the first direct government involvement in location decisions was important in the development of Ebbw Vale rather than Scunthorpe as the location for the first British strip mill (Warren 1970, 172–84). Since 1945 in steel development programmes, nationalization, denationalization, the controversy over the fourth strip mill in the late fifties, through to renationalization again in 1967, and with new rationalization programmes in the early 1970s, governments have played a major role in postwar location decisions. Later, on a smaller scale, but no less contentiously, government has become involved in shipbuilding

rationalization and shipyard preservation, first through the Geddes
Report of 1966, later through the Fairfields operation, the wider Upper
Clyde Shipbuilders, very heavily subsidized Harland and Wolff expansion
in Belfast, and by 1974 national ownership of the Doxford yards on the
Wear and, prospectively, general national ownership of shipbuilding and
repairing.

More generally, over the whole postwar period, but particularly from
the mid-sixties, financial incentives and concessions designed to bolster
the economy and society of the development areas has had a major
effect on the location of economic activity in Britain. In steel in particular, but also to some extent in chemicals, this has accentuated a division
of Britain into two regions—a north and west with primary trades including steelmaking and heavy engineering, the heavy chemical lines—and a
south east of Britain with new, lighter, growth industries, metalworking
rather than metal-making, light engineering for consumers rather than
capital markets, lighter higher-value chemical products. In short, there
is reason to suppose that the well-meaning efforts of governments of
both political persuasions have had unfortunate results. Concepts of the
'proper place' for heavy industry have helped to increase its already
strong concentration in the peripheral regions. Moreover, in aiming to
preserve employment government action has helped also to preserve too
many plants for optimum scales of operation and in locations which are
deficient. The rationalization which, however painful in the short run,
might have made British heavy industries internationally competitive
again, has not been pursued vigorously enough. The results have been a
continuous long-term decline in the British position in world heavy
industry, an international locational shift.

Until 1890 Britain was the world's leading steel producer: it lost its
lead in heavy chemicals later in that decade but in shipbuilding not until
1956. In 1972 Japanese shipyards launched ten times the tonnage of
British yards and Sweden and West Germany were also ahead. United
Kingdom sulphuric acid production is not only exceeded by that of the
United States and U.S.S.R. but also by that of Japan, Germany, and
France. In 1973 Britain was fifth in world steel output but made only
3·8 per cent of the total tonnage. Location is only one of the complex of
factors accounting for the undoubted malaise of the British economy at
the beginning of the final quarter of the twentieth century, but it is a not
unimportant one. An important lesson of the study of the past geography
of British heavy industry is that radical change is difficult to secure:
another, even more critical, is that radical changes are the only ones
which have a chance of success in the end.

References

Aberconway, Lord (1927) *The Basic Industries of Great Britain*, London.

Abercrombie, P. and Archibold, J. (1925) *East Kent Regional Planning Scheme, Preliminary Survey*, 38.

Addis, J. P. (1957) *The Crawshay Dynasty*.

Allen, G. C. (1929) *The Industrial Development of Birmingham and the Black Country*.

Armstrong, W. G. (ed.) (1864) *The Industrial Resources of the Tyne, Wear and Tees*, Newcastle upon Tyne.

Bailey, S. C. (1861) *Transactions of the North of England Institute of Mining Engineers*, x, 29.

Barlow, M. (1940) *Royal Commission on the Distribution of the Industrial Population*, Report and Minutes of Evidence.

Bauerman, H. (1874) *Metallurgy*, 12, 229, 223.

Bell Brothers, *Minute Books*, British Steel Corporation Record Office, Middlesbrough.

Bell, Sir H. (1903) *The Times*, 3 December.

Bellerby, J. R. (1943) *Economic Reconstruction: A Study of Post War Problems*, 159.

Bessborough, Lord (ed.) (1950) *Lady Charlotte Guest. Extracts from her Journal. 1833–1852*, 66.

Billy and Melius (1904) Articles in *Iron Age* on 'British Iron and Steel Districts'.

Brassey, T. (1879) 'The Depression of Trade', *The Nineteenth Century Magazine*, 795.

British Iron Trade Association (1896), (1) *The Iron and Steel Industries of Belgium and Germany*. (2) Annual Meeting: speech by Alfred Hickman, President.

Bruce, H. A. (1853) letter in *Dowlais Company Records*, Section C, Box 8, Cardiff Record Office.

Burn, D. L. (1940) *The Economic History of Steelmaking 1867–1939*.
– (1961) *The Steel Industry 1939–1959*.

Cambell, W. A. (c. 1965) *The Old Tyneside Chemical Trades*.

Carr, J. C. and Taplin, C. (1962) *History of the British Steel Industry*.

Carvell, J. L. (1948) *The Coltness Iron Company*.

Cassell and Co. (1882) *Great Industries of Great Britain*, 3 vols.

Chemical Trade Journal (1888), 3 November, 275.
– (1896), 21 March.
– (1897), 3 April, 234.
– (1899), 18 February, 128.

Civil Engineers (1887) *Proceedings of the Institute*, 88, 439.

Colliery Guardian (1863), 16 May, 394.
– (1868), 21 March, 269.
– (1873), 28 March, 372–3.
– (1879), 25 April, 656.
– (1880), 9 July, 66.
– (1882), 5 May, 707–8.

Collins, L. and Walker, D. F. (eds.) (1975) *Locational Dynamics of Manufacturing Industry*, London.

Comprehensive Gazeteer of England and Wales (1895), London.

Conzen, M. R. G. (1958) on 'Shipbuilding' in Daysh, G. H. J., *A Survey of Whitby and the Surrounding Area*, 59–72.

Cowper, E. A. (1865) in *British Association Reports,* 177.
Day, St. John (1876) 'The Iron and Steel Industries' in *Notices on Some of the principle manufactures of the West of Scotland,* British Association, 5.
Depression of Trade and Industry (1886) *Royal Commission.* Evidence of S. Osborn, 2nd Rep. Questions 3278–80; A. Hewlett 3rd Rep. 205; 2nd Rep. Replies to circular to Chambers of Commerce 390/1.
Dunbar, R. H. (1882) 'Sir John Brown' in *Great Industries of Great Britain,* 1, 286.
Dupin, C. (1826) *Force commerciale de la Grande Bretagne,* 5, 227–8.
Encyclopaedia Britannica (1877 and 1902) articles on Darlington.
Engineer (1876), 1 December, 473.
– (1889), 29 November, 621.
– (1895), 20 September, 296.
– (1903), 26 June, 662.
Erickson, C. (1959) *British Industrialists: steel and hosiery 1850–1950.*
Glasgow Herald (1938) *Trade Review,* 29 December, 33.
Gossage, W. (1861) 'On the History of the Alkali Manufacture', *British Association Report,* Liverpool Meeting, 81.
Grunner and Lan, (1861) Reports on British ironworks in *Annales des mines,* 5th Ser., xx, 542.
Grunner and Lan (1863) in the *Mining and Smelting Magazine,* 13.
Hall, J. (1857) *The Iron Question considered in connection with theory, practice and experiment with special reference to the Bessemer process,* London.
Hall, P. (ed.) (1966) *Von Thunen's Isolated State,* trans. C. M. Wartenberg, New York.
Hallsworth, H. H. (1935) The Shipbuilding Industry in Jones, J. H., *Britain in Depression,* 251–2.
Hamilton, E. (1920) to Bolckow and Vaughan A. G. M., *The Economist,* 2 October, 521.
Harmsworth (*c.* 1907) *Atlas and Gazeteer,* 1.
Hartshorne (1939) *The Nature of Geography,* 419.
Heal, D. (1974) *The Steel Industry in Post War Britain.*
Hewitt, A. (1868) 'The Production of Iron and Steel in its Economic and Social Relations', *Official Report on the Paris Exposition.*
Hibbs, C. (1882) in *Great Industries of Great Britain,* iii, 187.
Hogg, I. (1958) excursion, British Association, Glasgow.
Hull, E. C. (1862) 'The Lancashire Coalfield', *Colliery Guardian,* 8 February, 103.
I.D.A.C. (1937) *Report of the Import Duties Advisory Committee,* 51.
Imperial Gazeteer (1874), Edinburgh.
Imperial Gazeteer of England and Wales (1872), Edinburgh.
Iron (1875), 5 June, 717.
– (1882), 6 January, 5.
– (1884), 6 June, 499.
Iron and Coal Trades Review (1882), 24 November, 576.
– (1886), 12 February, 238.
– (1887), 18 November, 739.
– (1888), (1) 27 July, 132; (2) 3 August, 166.
– (1907), 8 February, 451–5.
Iron and Steel Institute (1935) *Iron, Steel and Engineering Industries of Manchester and District.*
Jeans, J. S. (1902) *American Industrial Conditions and Competition,* Chapter 8.
Jones, L. (1957) *Shipbuilding in Britain.*
Journal of the Iron and Steel Institute (1871), August.
Journal of the Society of Chemical Industry (1905), 16 January, 19.
Kirchhoff, C. (1900) *Notes on Some European Iron Making Districts,* 84.
Levy, H. (1927) *Monopolies, Cartels and Trusts in British Industry,* 194–6.
Lewis (1848) *Topographical Dictionary of England.*
– (1848) *Topographical Dictionary of Wales.*

Littlewood, D. (1962–3) unpublished M.A. thesis on *The British Automobile Industry to 1938*, University of Leicester.

Lunge, G. (1893) 'The education of industrial chemists', *Chemical Trade Journal*, 16 December, 387.

Macarthur, J. (1890) *New Monkland Parish: Its History, Industries and People.*

McCord, N. and Rowe, D. J. (1971) *Northumberland and Durham, An Industrial Miscellany*, Newcastle, 28.

Macrosty, H. W. (1907) *The Trust Movement in British Industry*, 66.

McCulloch, J. R. (1839) *Statistical Account of the British Empire*, ii, 67.

– (1866) *A Dictionary Geographical, Statistical and Historical*, ii.

Marshall, J. D. (1958) *Furness and the Industrial Revolution.*

Marx, K. (1845) *Eleven Theses on Fuerbach*, quoted B. Russell in *A History of Western Philosophy* (1946), 811.

Mattox, W. S. (1898) 'The Black Country' in *Iron Age*, 27 October, 14.

Meade, R. (1882) *The Coal and Iron Industries of the United Kingdom.*

Mechanics Magazine (1861), 16 August, 95.

Menelaus, W. (1857) Report to G. T. Clark on Dowlais Works, *Dowlais Papers*, Section C, Box 8, Cardiff Record Office.

Mineral Statistics of the United Kingdom (1890).

Mining Journal (1850), 16 March.

– (1853), 4 June.

Morris, J. H. and Williams, L. J. (1958) *The South Wales Coal Industry 1841– 1875*, 90.

National Cyclopaedia (1847–51), London.

Nevins, A. (1935) *Abram S. Hewitt*, 35, 36.

North Eastern Gazette (1869), 19 November, editorial 'Salt–a new local industry'.

Parkinson J. R. (1960) *The Economics of Shipbuilding in the United Kingdom.*

Price, J. (1886) *Royal Commission on Depression of Trade and Industry*, Parliamentary Papers 1886, xxii, 149.

Railway Agreements and Amalgamations (1911) *Departmental Committee* on 312.

Railway Rates Tribunal (1911) 25.

Ramsden, J. (1897) Obituary Notice, *Proceedings Institute of Civil Engineers*, 129, 385–97.

Renner, G. T. (1947) 'Geography of Industrial Localisation', *Economic Geography*, 23, 167–89.

Richardson, T. and Watts, H. (1863) *Chemical Technology.*

Royal Geographical Society (1938) *Journal*, xcii, 22–39, 499–526.

Ruskin, J. (1907) 'Ad Valorem' in *Unto this Last* (1859–60), Cassell edition, 195.

Rylands (1890 and 1906) *Rylands Directory of the Iron, Steel, Coal and Allied Trades* (published triennially since 1882).

Samuelson, F. (1922) Presidential Address, *Journal of the Iron and Steel Institute*, 1, 47.

Skelton, H. J. (1912) letter to *The Times*, 27 February.

S.M.I. (1947) *Sheet Metal Industries*, December, 2447.

Smith, D. M. (1971) *Industrial Location: An Economic Geographical Analysis*, New York.

Society of Arts (1860) *Journal*, 3 August, 685.

Special Committee on Iron (1861–2) *Transaction and Report*, 1.

Stainton, J. H. (1924) *The Making of Sheffield 1865–1914*, 5.

Thorpe, T. E. (1895) Presidential Address, *Journal of the Society of Chemical Industry*, 28 February.

U.A.C. *United Alkali Company Records* at Imperial Chemical House.

– (1890) *Prospectus of the United Alkali Company.*

Vaizey, J. (1974) *History of the British Steel Industry.*

Wallwork, K. L. (1974) *Derelict Land*, Newton Abbot.

Warren, K. (1969) 'Iron and Steel in North East England; Regional Implications of development in a basic industry', *Regional Studies*, 3 (1), 49–60.

Warren, K. (1970) *The British Iron and Steel Sheet Industry since 1840: an Economic Geography*, London, 223, 224, 231.
– (1973) *North East England* (Problem Regions of Europe Series), 34–6.
Weber, A. (1929) *Theory of the Location of Industries*, trans. C. J. Friedrich, Chicago.
Weldon, W. (1884) *Journal of the Society of Chemical Industry*, 29 July, 387.
Westmacott, P. and Spencer, J. F. (1863) 'The Engineering Manufactures of the Tyne, Wear and Tees', *Colliery Guardian*, 31 October and 7 November.
Wilkie, G. (1857) *The Manufacture of Iron in Great Britain.*
Wilkins, C. (1903) *The History of the Iron, Steel, Tinplate and Other Trades of Wales*, Merthyr Tydfil, 63, 68.
Williams, D. (1796) *History of Monmouthshire.*

Further Reading

Ashton, T. S. (1948) *The Industrial Revolution 1760–1830*, London.
British Association. Reports of Annual Meetings; Regional Handbooks produced by local committees since early meetings.
Chambers, J. D. (1961) *The Workshop of the World, British Economic History 1820–1880.*
Clapham, Sir John (1926) *An Economic History of Modern Britain*, 3 vols.
Court, W. H. B. (1954) *A Concise Economic History of England since 1750.*
Darby, H. C. (1974) *A New Historical Geography of England.*
Hobsbawn, E. J. (1969) *Industry and Empire. The Economic History of Britain*, 3.
Jones, G. P. and Pool, A. G. (1940) *A Hundred Years of Economic Development in Great Britain (1840–1940).*
Landes, D. S. (1969) *The Unbound Prometheus.*
Lawton, R. (1964) 'Historical Geography: The Industrial Revolution' in Watson, J. W. and Sissons, J. B., *The British Isles: a systematic geography.*
Mumford, L. (1934) *Technics and Civilisation.*
Postan, M. and Habakkuk, H. J. (eds.) (1966) *The Cambridge Economic History of Europe* vol. vi, *The Industrial Revolution and After* (contains excellent bibliography).
Smith, W. (1949) *An Economic Geography of Britain.*
Ure, A. (1835 and 1861) *The Philosophy of Manufactures.*

Parliamentary Papers especially:

Royal Commission on the Depression of Trade and Industry 1886, Reports and Minutes of Evidence.
Committee on Industry and Trade (1927–9) (Balfour Committee), Reports and Minutes of Evidence.
Royal Commission on the Distribution of Industrial Population (1940) (The Barlow Commission), Report and Minutes of Evidence.

Journals

The Engineer.
Engineering.
Journal of the Royal Statistical Society.
Journal of the Society of Arts.
The *Mining Journal.*
Transactions of the National Association for the Promotion of Social Science (valuable reports on industries in regions of annual meetings).

Maps and Atlases

Ordnance Survey 1 in. and 6 in. series, various editions.
Bartholomew, J. G. (1899) *The Royal Atlas of England and Wales.*
– (1903) *The Survey Atlas of England and Wales.*
– (1907) *Atlas of the World's Commerce.*

Index